RED WINGS THROUGH THE FOREST

By
Tim Stanton

WORDS MATTER

P U B L I S H I N G

OUR WORDS CHANGE THE WORLD

Words Matter Publishing
P.O. Box 531
Salem, Il 62881
www.wordsmatterpublishing.com

ISBN 13: 978-1-953912-29-9

Library of Congress Catalog Card Number: 2021946326

DEDICATION

I dedicate this project to my forest of kids:
Justin, Holly, Aaron, Kyle, Kael, and Devin.
Most of all I thank God for trusting me with the
care of His beautiful creation, the forest.

TABLE OF CONTENT

RED WINGS THROUGH THE FOREST

Why name a book Red Wings Through the Forest? My Red Wing boots and I have hiked across the Missouri Ozarks for close to 40 years. They have visited every state west of Missouri. They have waded creeks and stomped out fires. Red Wing Boots have enabled me to do my job with comfort and confidence. In writing this book I am letting my boots do the talking; please come along for the hike as we travel through the woods, fight fire and meet some amazing folks along the way.

I was raised in the suburbs of Kansas City. There are not many opportunities for kids to be exposed to the great outdoors such as forests, lakes, fish, and wildlife while growing up in the city. I was blessed to have a father that was raised in rural north Missouri, near the Iowa line. It was his love and deep appreciation of his outdoor adventures, that made a forever impact on my life. My father made it a point to expose me to wildlife opportunities outside of the city via camping, hunting, and fishing. More importantly he shared with me an outdoor ethic. He gave me an appreciation for the natural world.

The inspiration for this book is to encourage grandparents and parents to engage with children to instill a love and respect for our great outdoors. Here I am at the age of 64 and because of the devotion my father had in exposing me to natural activities available in our beautiful state I still have a deep awareness for the land given to us by God. It is up to us to start the conversation with our youth about our resources, so they have a deeper responsibility to make a positive impact on the land. In Genesis 1:28 (KJV) it is written: "And God blessed them, and God said unto them, be fruitful, and multiply, and replenish the earth, and subdue it: and have dominion over the fish of the sea, and over the fowl of the air, and over every living thing that moves upon the earth."

When I made the decision to be a forester, I took great responsibility to ensure that our forests were kept in the best conditions. Healthy forests are needed to ensure that living creatures have the habitat required for survival, the lumber industry can meet the needs for the population in the United States and individuals can enjoy recreational hiking and hunting opportunities.

As with many other high school seniors I did not have a clue what I really wanted to be when I grew up. I knew I wanted an occupation that would allow me to work outside. My first year of college I went to Rockhurst College in Kansas City. There I was able to play on the varsity baseball team and take my basic college courses. While I was torn between my love of baseball and a career in the woods, I had to make a critical decision. Continue my education at Rockhurst and major in business or transfer to a college where I could gain a degree in a field that related to the great outdoors. The latter triumphed, and I transferred to the University of Missouri in Columbia. I obtained my degree in Forest Management in December of 1979. At that time my degree had only a hiring rate of 26%. Therefore, I was extremely grateful that in only 3 weeks from graduation I was hired by the Missouri Department of Conservation (MDC). MDC had just recently received a new tax initiative voted on and approved by the citizens of Missouri. This tax revenue allowed MDC to hire more employees and offer additional resources and programs to the people of Missouri.

As a forester with MDC I was blessed with a 34-year career and then continued as a contracted safety officer for Western Fire Detail another 6 years. I also taught forestry classes for Missouri State University and was the Safety Manager for Chloeta Fire out of Oklahoma. Through the years a goal of mine was to write a book to inspire individuals in what the forest has to offer, give a contribution to a scholarship program for high school seniors that want to achieve a degree in forestry. My intent is to share real life stories with you that will span through the forests of Missouri and all states west of Missouri.

Smoke and destruction from fire out west.
Photo Credit: Tim Stanton

Photo Credit: Tim Stanton

Sometimes colored fire retardant dropped from helicopter is necessary.

Photo Credit: Tim Stanton

Many thanks go out to those that helped with this project! Mark Masters, Chet Dodrill, and Alex Combo at:

Thank you, Missouri Department of Conservation for my dream career. Thank you for the pictures, Rick Bucannon Photos, Greg Hoss and Brad Jump. For helping me write these memories Valerie Stanton, Gwen Stanton, Nicole and Diane at Ava Place. Thank you, Stan Lovan for the encouragement to write everything down again, after my computer crashed. Thank you, Bob Frakes for steering me to publishers Words Matter Publishing and Tammy Koelling for taking my work and making it into a book.

It's been a great trip.

PART I

Forestry

*'We abuse land because we see it as
a commodity belonging to us. When we see land as
a community to which we belong, we may begin
to use it with love and respect.'*

– Aldo Leopold

BURR OAK

Burr Oak Woods, located in Blue Springs, MO, was a great place for me to start my career. It had just recently been purchased by Missouri Department of Conservation (MDC) for an urban public forest. The property was 700 acres in size, made up of forest and open fields. There was a sizable deer herd on the property as well. Prior to MDC ownership a developer had expressed interest in it for developing a subdivision. MDC's initial plans were to get it open to the public as quickly as possible.

Dennis, a newly hired forester from Utah, and I were there to "build" parking areas and hiking trails. We put up signs and cut down hazardous trees (trees that were dead, dying, or thorny). In the spring came tree planting. There were large open fields of fescue, a grass that is used for raising livestock but not good for wildlife. The fescue was removed, and wildlife friendly grasses were seeded. Dennis and I planted tree seedlings in these fields as well. The small seedling trees were acquired from the state nursery and were planted by hand and tractor.

Dennis and I were planting White Pine seedlings by hand and around noon we broke for lunch. One good thing about being a forester is you get to picnic every day. We sat down on a log in the shade and something caught my attention. About 6 inches from my boot was a large morel mushroom! As I bent down to pick it, I noticed there were mushrooms everywhere. For those of you that are not familiar with these natural treasures, morel mushrooms are highly sought after in hardwood forests. Later in my career I saw a sign in a health food store offering to buy morels for $80 per pound. Their value is in their flavor when deep fried in cooking oil. Dennis and I instantly changed our priorities and began picking mushrooms. Nearly all of them were as big as our fist. We filled up a 5 gallon cooler and our lunch boxes. After work we took our haul home for some fine dining.

Another funny story involved my co-worker Dennis, myself and a young lady applying for the secretarial job in the days of the new office. Our supervisor (who was going to be out for the day) had asked us to stay close to the office as applicants for the position of secretary were coming by and he wanted us to interview them, laying out a format for us to follow. The first applicant that came in was exceedingly beautiful and without saying a word we knew she was the one for the job. (Dennis and I were both single at the time.) The first order of business as laid out in the instructions was a typing test (on a typewriter). We handed her the standard format that she was to follow, and she looked at it, glanced at the typewriter and asked, "where is the W?" We were devastated.

Dennis and I were at Burr Oak for 2 and half years before Dennis was promoted to an office in Clinton, MO. A year later I was approached by a supervisor from Jefferson City and asked if I was interested in a promotion to Alton, Missouri. I said, "Yes, where is Alton, MO?" That last year I planted white pine, cleared out the underbrush and marked trails. The White Pine Plantation at Burr Oak is still there today providing a beautiful back drop for pictures and weddings. I do not know about the mushrooms.

Burr Oak 2020
Photo Credit: Gwen Stanton

ALTON, MO

Knowing why a forester is necessary goes back to the history of forestry in Missouri. Southern Missouri attracted settlers in the 1880's. To survive the ruggedness of the land they had to carve out an opening in the virgin forest. Next, build a home without modern equipment and create pasture and gardens for raising food. Envision with me for a moment an untouched landscape filled with trees. The settlers used crosscut saws and fire to accomplish the tasks at hand. Generations grew up with the mindset that one could set a fire with no intent of putting it out. The theory was simple, the more trees that died from fire meant less cutting with the crosscut saw. The forest was viewed as an obstacle to the early settlers.

In 1890 the largest sawmill in the United States (and possibly the world) was in Grandin, Southeast Missouri. To complement the sawmill, they also build bunk houses, a post office, a general store, doctor's office, a church and a saloon. Their objective was to provide railroad ties for the trans-continental railroad and oak construction lumber. By 1910, all of the mature lumber was gone from a 50-mile radius of the mill. Settlers moved back to the area and burned off the land to clean it up and stake their claim. This

30-year period changed the tree species composition. The non-merchantable (weed-tree) Blackjack oak is fire tolerant and took over the southwest hillsides where black and white oak had once stood. Blackjack, even though fire tolerant, is not usable for forest products. Missouri foresters then and now had to work around the Blackjack to reestablish the much preferred white and black oak. The history of Missouri forestry is imbedded in the upcoming stories that have molded my career.

My first assignment in southern Missouri brought my Red Wings to Alton. I moved from a population of 1 million to 702 people. It was a big shock to the system as I now had a party line for a telephone and one TV channel out of Arkansas. I quickly discovered the gifts of nature available to me that I had never seen before. The majestic Shortleaf Pine captured my heart. The pictures in textbooks did them no justice. The Eleven Point River rushes through the pine and oak with beauty, speed and grace with an abundance of trout and small mouth bass. The surrounding hillsides look much the same as when the first settlers saw them. Who needs TV when you have this to look at? However, the party line was difficult to get used to!

Coming from the big city, I was conditioned to work according to the clock. If I had an appointment for 10:15 am, I showed up at 10:00 am. That did not always work for me in Oregon County. I had a forest owner call and ask me to come to his property and look at his timber on Thursday evening. I said I am off work at 5:00. Quite puzzled with my response he replied, "I said tomorrow evening, you know 2:00 or 3:00." I found out that there were only two times per day, morning, and evening. With this system they wouldn't have to be tied to a clock and they would have more time for fishing, hunting, talking, or any of their other priorities.

They also found a way to beef up adjectives. If something was really good, it was "fine right"! Or if bad. it was "bad right"! Hold on, my Oregon County friends. I am not making fun of you. It made me realize that I was the square peg trying to fit into the round hole, so it was me that needed to round off my rough edges to fit in. It did not take long, either. Shortly after arriving I called my mom back home in Kansas City. She could not believe how much her son's vocabulary and speech had changed. I carried this principal with me throughout the Ozarks.

One fine-right story that is imprinted in my mind is the time that Rob and Al, friends of mine and avid fishermen, were excited about a day long float trip on the popular Eleven Point River. They unloaded at the boat ramp and shoved off for a day full of fishing and canoeing. They got about 3 miles downriver and Al asked Rob, "Did we move the truck off the boat ramp and into a parking space?" Oops, in their excitement their truck was still on the ramp, and worse yet keys still in the ignition and it was running. The thought of paddling back was quickly squelched as the current was far too aggressive, making that endeavor impossible. This was in days before cell phones, and their fun trip was now overshadowed by the possibility of their vehicle being stolen. They decided to make the best out of it, continued fishing and made the float trip as enjoyable as possible. Luckily for them, a forest-service law enforcement person found their truck and moved it to the parking lot. Rob and Al's wives met them at the end of the float and delivered them back to their truck.

The locals get a kick out of the city folk when they would float the river for the first time. There is a spot where they congregate with lawn chairs, beverages, lunch and just sit and watch, waiting for the inexperienced floaters to navigate this particular rapid. This was a great source of their entertainment. But it could be lucrative as well. As soon as the canoes were upright and back on the river the locals would wait out to see if any loot was left behind. I unfortunately was not a spectator for these events, but a floater/flipper on one of the occasions.

Conservation agents, also known as game wardens, are employed by MDC as well. An agent's responsibility is to enforce all the Conservation laws to ensure that all the state land and resources owned by MDC are protected. An agent must have a bachelor's degree and go through the department's six-month law enforcement program. One Saturday MDC's Conservation Agents were asked by the Federal Wildlife Enforcement Officers to help them conduct some surveillance along the Eleven Point River. Since the Eleven Point River went through Mark Twain National Forest it was the responsibility on the federal side to investigate and keep the waterway safe and clean. There had been many complaints that heavy drinking, drugs, littering and just overall orneriness was taking place on the river. For me as a forester to have a better understanding as to the agent's job, I was asked to tag along. We met up with other local, state and federal agents early so that we could be in position before most of the public were canoeing on the river. Around ten in the morning we spotted a group that was already obviously drunk. (This was the group that Gary and I were tasked to follow). We stayed back and floated behind them. As they came to a holler beside the river, they parked their canoes and started walking through the woods. When we came up on their abandoned canoes, we floated a little farther down the river and hiked back to their location. Gary motioned me to stop. Just ahead of us was a man and woman in waist deep grass doing the "wild thing." Since that isn't technically illegal, we had to stay hidden until they were done and joined back up with their fellow floaters. We sleuthed to a great place to hunker down and watch the entire party. We were so well hidden that one of the men in the group literally came within a few feet of us to relieve himself. Because we were well hidden, or he was very drunk, whichever, we were lucky not to get sprayed. They partied around a campfire and it was not long before they began passing something around with each taking a "hit" off the little white object. This is when Gary gave me the signal and we approached the party. (All other agents were following other parties, so it was just Gary and I at this location.) It was quite the scene, and it is fine with me that I never had to do that again! The little white objects were confiscated, and the floaters were issued tickets for any and all of their illegal activities. They could continue their float but with the nuisance now of having to pay the fine or return to court.

I have always been an advocate of education and additional training whenever it was presented to me. I had the opportunity while living in Alton to participate in an extensive Timber Stand Improvement (TSI) training exercise conducted by MDC. A TSI is a timber management tool to reduce the low-quality trees so that the higher quality trees will grow faster, thus producing more board feet and better-quality lumber. The University of Missouri had originated the research project in the '50's on a 40-acre plot owned by the university. There were 4 plots each being 10 acres and relatively the same amount of timber on each plot. One plot was left untouched: the control plot. The second plot received a light cutting of TSI. The third plot received a medium cutting of TSI, while the fourth plot received a heavy cutting of TSI. In 1983 I was an assistant resource forester and all foresters with MDC were invited to participate in cutting the different plots so the timber could be evaluated. Part of the training exercise was to operate heavy equipment such as a skidder, loader, and chainsaws. MDC rented the equipment so that each forester had ample opportunity to learn the proper use of each tool. This type of equipment is used by large logging companies. It was our job to harvest all 4 plots; we cut all the trees on the plots by using chainsaws. The trees were then skidded to the loaders. The loaders placed the timber onto log trucks and delivered to a sawmill that was owned by the university. At the sawmill it was determined the amount of volume and quality of timber for each plot. Final results indicated that the medium TSI plot had the most volume of timber and the best quality of lumber. This information was relative for foresters since it proved that the best practice was to thin by using a medium TSI methodology. I have used the knowledge of this training over my 30-plus-year career in educating landowners that this type of TSI was the best practice for their land if their objective was to produce quality timber. TSI is the best tool to manage timber, reference to which is throughout this book.

Oregon County is blessed with many natural resources. MDC foresters assist landowners with managing their forest land. The demand for forest products requires that we grow trees to maturity as quickly as possible. Growing trees is like growing a garden. In a garden you want your vegetables to grow as fast and as big as possible. You do this by removing the weeds, so all the sunlight, moisture, and nutrients go to the vegetables. Such is the same in a forest. The weed trees are the low value trees that are of poor species, diseased, crooked, or damaged. By removing these trees, more sunlight, moisture, and nutrients go to the highest quality trees. This will accelerate their growth. The weed-trees that are cut usually have little or no value other than firewood or charcoal. These "cull" trees can be piled up in the woods for wildlife cover as well. I have seen many turkey nests in such brush piles.

It is also great cover for a rabbit to escape a coyote. The process in removing weed-trees when TSI is implemented correctly will mature trees 20-30 years quicker and be of better quality.

In closing out the section on Alton I want to take a moment and give a shout out to my Oregon county friends. It was here that I learned how to be a pig farmer, killed my first turkey, added to my vocabulary, witnessed neighbors helping neighbors, managed my first timber sale, had my first fire season, and did my first Smokey Bear programs. Not bad for this kid from Kansas City. Most importantly, this is when I accepted Christ as my savior, added to my family my beautiful daughter, and made very special lifetime friends. I rounded off my rough "city" edges and found I could fit in here just fine.

Ava, MO

In 1984 I was promoted to Resource Forester and relocated my family to Ava, MO. We moved in January and wow it was cold! My young family and I moved into a unique home with no heat (wood burning furnace and no firewood the first night) and our furniture still in route. We put on the long johns and cuddled together in the living room.

Now, I would be serving Douglas and Ozark counties during my tenure as a resource forester. (This county was 60% forested, including my beloved shortleaf pine.) This new role I had been given included the responsibilities to supervise 3 to 5 employees and oversee the physical office located in Ava. The resource forester assists landowners with managing their forest as well as fire suppression and fire prevention.

I had only met this work team on one other occasion and therefore I knew little about them. Stan and Chuck (nearing retirement) were the longest running employees of this office and Francis was there at the time as well. On my first day of work, I walked out of my office and into the shop. Chuck walked over to a cabinet and pulled out a glass bottle containing a brown liquid, took a big swallow, and put the bottle back. I did not say anything. Chuck walked out of the office and Stan walked in. I asked Stan if Chuck had a drinking problem and I told hm what I had seen. Stan laughed and laughed and managed to say, "Chuck was ornery and was trying to get a reaction out of you." After everyone left for the day, I checked the bottle and found it full of tea. The next morning, I got there first and when Chuck walked in and I went over to the cabinet and took a swig of the bottle. I put the bottle up and gave him a wink. I passed the test!

On another occasion, Chuck was asked to go to the Regional Office in West Plains to put a new roof on the large storage building. When Chuck got there, he walked into the Regional Supervisor's office and told the supervisor he had a doctor's appointment and would have to leave at 2:00 pm. There was a crew of eight on the roof in the hot sun. Everyone was in a bad mood due to the heat. Chuck had not told anyone other than the supervisor that he was leaving at 2:00. When 2:00 came around, Chuck stood up and dropped his roofing hammer and simply said, "I have had enough, I am leaving", which he did. As soon as his truck left the parking lot the rest of the crew went into the supervisor's office, tattling. Chuck got the last laugh, he always did. He was a great employee for me, as a new supervisor. He made me ask questions and be specific. Chuck and I got off on a good start and he kept me on my toes.

Douglas and Ozark Counties have diverse landscapes. The east 2/3 of the county contains quality oak and shortleaf pine. The western 1/3 is mostly open grass land. The US Forest Service owns a large piece of the eastern grasslands and this area has been designated as a state natural area and a scenic byway.

The Ozark Mountains and crystal clear, spring fed streams provide beautiful landscapes and a home for a variety of wildlife. These mountains may not be as majestic as the Rockies or the Smokey Mountains, but the charm in this smaller mountain range takes up mostly Ozark County and a smaller portion of Douglas County with rich oak hickory and shortleaf pine.

The Forestry Division assists with forest management of both timber and wildlife. The service is free to landowners and thankfully many use these services to improve their land. Landowners that take advantage of our assistance have a great appreciation for natural resources. Sometimes the landowner does not see the benefits of forest management. For example, it can take an oak, without management, over 100 years to mature. With management, it will take oak trees 65 to 75 years to mature. Responsible private landowners use The Forestry Division resources for their timber management because it is the right thing to do.

Unfortunately, the current trend does not include private land forest management. The older generation has a strong interest in tithing the natural resources. As this older generation passes on their private forest land to their sons and daughters, many times the interest is not there. Many, not all, young people today are wired to the indoors. Richard Louv coined the phrase "Nature-Deficit Disorder" in a publication entitled "Last Child in the Woods: Saving Our Children from Nature-Deficit Disorder." He discusses today's youth problems as rooted in the fact that they do not go outside to unwind. Instead their brains are in constant electronic stimulation. It also leads to a trend of offspring liquidating their deceased parent forest land. It is also common throughout the US, enrollment for Forestry degrees is down by as much as 90% in some schools. A major hurdle for future foresters.

There is a large ranch in Ozark County named Pleasant Ranch. Its name is appropriate for the beautiful cattle pastures, lake, and timber. The owner's name was also "Pleasant," and that description rings true of the entire family's personality. I had worked with the Pleasants on several occasions but I especially recall one job where I was asked to assess a potential timber sale.

On the appointed day I drove through their large gate that proudly exhibited their name. As I got closer to their stables, I could see Danny Pleasant and his father, Gene, saddling up three horses. This was very alarming to me as I am not a horse lover. Do not get me wrong, I think they are beautiful animals, but I do not like crawling on the back of an animal that has a mind of its own. On past visits to their property, we had always taken the ATV's through the woods. I like ATV's!! Call me a control freak.

Gene was already stepping up on a trailer to get on his horse due to bad knees. Danny threw himself on his horse in cowboy fashion, leaving the third horse glaring me down. As I approached the horse, I could see it was a pregnant mare about as wide as a pickup truck. I looked at Danny to see if he was smiling at this joke and he was not. I climbed on to that wide load and quickly found out we had something in common, our dislike for each other!

As the three of us trotted into the woods I quickly found out that my horse knew her tree species. Blackjack Oak is the only Missouri oak that does not self-prune. It holds onto its stout dead branches. The horse vigorously tried to knock me off at every Blackjack Oak in that forest. I blindly rode through the forest trying to keep the branches from poking my eyes out and I missed the beautiful sights I so greatly appreciate.

We got to the bottom of the hill and a creek bank. Blackjack does not grow in bottomland soils, so I got a break until my horse discovered a greenbrier bush. (You know that wad of bush armed with sharp thorns.) Now I had sharp thorns instead of dead branches. Finally, we went beside the creek and found some mature Black and White Oak that needed harvesting. Danny rode off to check on some cattle while Gene and I kept riding along the creek. Gene stopped suddenly because his horse had gotten his rear leg caught in a large grape vine. Remember, Gene had to have the assistance of a trailer to get on and off his horse. That means I had to slide off of my horse and try to untangle the back-left hoof of Gene's. Anyone that has ever been around horses knows the pain of being kicked by a hind leg containing a steel horseshoe. Luckily for me Gene rode a well-mannered horse. After a few nervous minutes, I had them untangled and I sprawled back onto my horse. We rode back to the stables through my favorite Blackjack trees, grateful this exploration was about over!

I made the plans for marking the trees with paint for the loggers to cut. I told them I would draw up a contract between the loggers and the Pleasants and get it out to them later in the week. This is the only project I ever did on horseback and was happy to drive off into the sunset in my truck. On a side note, I could not walk without pain for four days after.

Tucked away in the heart of Douglas County is a Catholic Monastery, Our Lady of the Assumption Abbey, surrounded by forest. This abbey had 3,000 acres of oak and shortleaf pine. The beautiful Bryant Creek flowed through the property. Prior to the 1970's the monks were a "silent order" and could not talk until promoted to the next level. They had to be self-sufficient and they did so by making and selling concrete construction blocks. At that time, the monks wore sandals and long robes which would also be worn while helping MDC fight fire.

By the time I arrived in Douglas County, there were two major changes. They all could talk, and they now made fruit cakes instead of cement blocks. Some would say there is not much difference between a fruit cake and a concrete block, but these fruit cakes are very good, thanks to a French recipe. (I asked one of the monks how many fruit cakes they had sold. His reply: "Why all of them, of course.")

My main contact at the Monastery was Brother Boniface. At approximately 60 years old he stood proudly at 5'10 inches with a wiry build and leather skinned. Even though he could talk, he was a man of few words. Bonny was his nickname, trained in proper Timber Stand Improvement, and his assigned job was 50 acres of TSI each year. He cut out the "weed trees" so the best species and most vigorous and valuable trees had more room to grow. The abbey received reimbursement through a Federal Cost Share Program. Talk about job security, at 50 acres per year, it would take him 60 years to do the TSI for the whole property. It was up to me to verify that the work was done and to request the reimbursement. I have many Brother Bonny stories I could share; the man was that colorful. One afternoon we were hiking the property on a steep hill when he became quite winded. I asked if he needed to stop and rest for a minute. The response in his gruff monotone voice, "Why? Do you need to rest?" Another visit, he met me with his arm in a cast. I inquired about the mishap and he informed me a tree had fallen on him. But his injury did not stop the work, and we set out to look at some of the TSI he had done when he broke his arm. We came to a fence and even with his broken arm he climbed one side only to fall to the ground on the other side. Before I could inquire about his wellbeing colorful language flew from the Brother's mouth. I did not dare crack a smile, most times I did find the man a little intimidating.

The good Brother also was the abbey's forest fire department. He had a leaf rake and a backpack blower for equipment. The rake and blower are used to create a fire break by removing dry oak leaves, exposing bare ground all around the fire. That is all for now about my friend but remember my friend, Brother Bonny's name, for there will be more stories later in my fire section.

One of the most rewarding jobs a forester can do is tree planting. Many forestry practices take too long before you start seeing the fruits of your labor. Tree planting success only takes a year or two. We plant trees for windbreaks, wildlife food and cover, erosion control, post wildfire rehab, forest products and just for the beauty of it all.

Wilma Hutcheson, a long time Ava resident, came to my office with an idea to beautify the highway that runs through Ava. Her idea was to plant redbud and dogwood along Highway 5, from the north county line to the south county line. This was an aggressive idea for an 18-mile strip of trees. I was able to acquire an MDC grant and there were some donations. A solid line of trees was not doable, so we decided to place emphasis on the portion of highway going through Ava and random plantings north and south of town.

Mrs. Hutchison was successful in acquiring free prison labor to do the planting. My work team and I also helped with the planning, logistics and planting. Mrs. Hutchison did a great job of supervision and the convicts were delighted to be outside planting trees. I was planting trees with the convicts when Mrs. Hutchison was seen coming toward us. The young man beside me said to his inmates, "straighten up, here comes the mayor". That was the nickname they had for her, not in humor but in total respect for her passion for the project.

The project was successful. We had around 80% survival within Ava city limits. These trees were cared for by Ava City employees and volunteers. The survival rate outside of city limits decreased because they were on their own. Despite that, there are still enough to beautify the landscape.

Another MDC grant was acquired by Cathy Thompson when she was Ava Park Supervisor. The city park was virtually treeless except for a creek corridor and two pine trees planted in the '70's. The park today boasts of mature oak, Sycamore, and a variety of flowering species. The City followed up by planting some pine trees and I planted some pine at the park's ball field to compliment Cathy's idea.

The true measure of these projects' success is seen every Spring when the purple flowers of the Red Bud and white flowers of the Dogwood show off their beauty.

A private land forester deals with many landowners who have many different reasons for owning forest land. The number one reason is wildlife management because managing for forest products takes a lot of time. Many landowners inherit land and do not know anything about forest management.

Jack and Martha Ashbaugh were a forester's dream. In the 1950's Jack and Martha purchased 2,400 acres of land in Douglas County for less than $50 per acre. They lived in Georgia at the time but planned on moving to Missouri when they retired.

The first thing after purchasing the land Jack hired a local man named Stoney to watch over the property. He took the liberty to build a crude shack on the property to live in. Stoney's first job was to put up "NO TRESSPASSING" signs on the property. This made the local hunters mad and they set fire to the property. Stoney decided to paint "GAME WARDEN" on his truck. That was a bad idea as it made the locals angrier.

The burning continued for years but surprisingly did little damage to the timber. The Ashbaughs fired Stoney and built a home on their property. MDC fire fighters suggested that they should allow hunting by permission and see if that helped. MDC also loaned Jack a pump, tank, and hose that he could slide into his pickup. This would allow him to suppress small fires before they did any damage.

Jack and Martha started managing their timber and working with MDC foresters. They enrolled in the Forest Crop Land program which gave them a property tax break. The program required them to perform forest management practices. Jack hired contractors to do Timber Stand Improvement practices which planted trees and removed damaged or low value trees. By doing this, more sunlight, moisture and nutrients are supplied to the healthy trees.

The fires started to decline, and the timber growth began increasing. In 1983, the Ashbaughs were awarded the honor of being Tree Farmers of the Year. This award is only given to one landowner in Missouri per year.

When I moved to Ava in 1984 and began working with Jack and Martha, the first order of business was a public tour of their property to show other landowners that timber management works.

The Forest Crop Land Program is a 25-year program and for the Ashbaughs, that meant the program expired in 1984. They asked me to renew it for another 25 years. I began the process by pulling the Ashbaugh file. The file was 12 inches thick! I inventoried the entire 2600 acres and made some management recommendations. Jack exceeded my suggestions. He signed up for 50 acres of TSI per year. He also wanted to plant 10 acres of pine. He asked me to see if any of the property needed harvesting. I had never worked with or even heard of a forest landowner with such a passion. Jack, Martha, and I began a close working relationship that would last for years.

In 2007 Jack and Martha asked me to come to their home. They were both in their early 80's and they said they can no longer walk through their forest. They had two daughters that had no interest in owning the property because they were both married and had moved away. Jack asked if MDC would be interested in purchasing it for $360 per acre. In my mind I was thinking the land was worth twice that and had been properly managed. In addition to the land there was a ¼ mile of pristine Bryant Creek as a north boundary. Jack said he would also finance the sale over eight years. I said that I would pass his request up the channel, but I was sure there would be interest.

I introduced the purchase request to the Regional Planning committee and they unanimously agreed with me that MDC should purchase the property. The request was sent up to the Central Office. It is here that the Land Acquisition Committee had a dilemma. A large Fish Hatchery project was to take 5 years to complete. The contractor completed it in 3 years and demanded full payment at that time. This meant that there were no funds to purchase the Ashbaugh property.

I had to break the news to the Ashbaughs. They ended up selling the property on the open market with deed restrictions that all timber cutting would be done under the management of MDC. Jack had several offers but only one would agree to the restriction. The acquisition was completed.

Now for the bad news. This buyer did not lie but he also did not relay the whole truth. The buyer was a broker and immediately sold it to a corporation's retirement account that began cutting without management.

The cutting took place while the Ashbaughs were still living on the property and the cutting was going on around their home. It was not long before Jack died. Was it because of the cutting of the forest all around him? Nobody knows. Martha asked that I speak at Jack's funeral. For a visual aide I brought to the funeral the Ashbaugh file to show his dedication to our natural resources and I spoke of his environmental ethic and impact. It was not much later that Martha died as well.

This story does not end here on a sad note. The Missouri State Parks, an agency that deals more with outdoor recreation (hiking, camping, fishing, outdoor education) purchased the property and created a State Park. The cutting had only taken place on about ¼ of the property. The Ashbaugh legacy lives on.

While serving the communities of Douglas and Ozark Counties I was able to make significant contributions enriching the forest resources. My Red Wing boots have taken me thousands of miles over these two counties.

MDC manages both state-owned forests and privately-owned forests. There are more options when managing state land, but we assist private owners when possible.

There is an alternative living community (AKA Commune) in Ozark County that has around 2000 acres of timber land. The age of the residents run from teens to seniors, but most are in their 20's, just trying to "find themselves". I had heard that they were "clothing optional" but in my previous forest management visits I had seen none of that.

To manage a forest for timber products there must be some cutting, or the trees just grow old and die. To do nothing can be a management decision. It all depends on the landowner's objectives. On my previous visits to this property, their objective was the "do nothing" method to preserve their forest.

One summer day I met with the leader of the community and he said they were tired of living in tents, buses, and cars. They wanted to purchase a small sawmill and harvest the trees that needed to be removed to improve forest health. The lumber would be used to build structures. Wow, a great opportunity on a beautiful piece of land.

Now that I knew and agreed with their objective, I told him I would do a detailed survey of the property, develop a management plan, and then present my findings to the community. The leader gave me the okay.

I made three field visits to the property and gathered the data that I needed to construct a comprehensive management plan. On each trip there were fully clothed curiosity seekers following me around and asking questions. After completing the plan, I contacted the community leader and set up a time to present the plan to anyone that cared to listen. Bob, my supervisor, had called me and asked to go with me because he had never been there before.

We arrived at the appointed time of noon. The temperature was in the 90's. The leader was eating his lunch under the shade of a big white oak. There were two other guys there eating as well and I had no idea what they were eating and was glad they did not offer some to us. The leader said, "We will listen to the presentation right here." Of course, he was in the shade and I was in the sun. Bob was sitting on the bench to my left. A crowd started walking in and carrying lawn chairs.

I began with introductions and describing the purpose of my visit. I happened to look at Bob and he had this strange look on his face while looking to my right. As I continued my presentation I glanced to my right and there was a well-endowed, topless, young lady. I knew for certain that I could never again look right if I was going to finish this presentation. Without skipping a beat, I turned my attention toward my left. It was there I discovered another shirtless young lady breastfeeding her large toddler. I now could no longer look left. I finished the rest of the presentation looking straight at the community leader.

Bob later told me that he was in awe that I never missed a beat during the presentation. (Secretly, so was I). They never taught us this at our Instructor Training Class. Unfortunately, I did not get to see this project through as my days in the Ava office were numbered. But I did hear that my plans were approved, and the project was completed.

MDC manages many of the natural resources in the state. The beautiful rivers and streams are very popular with vacationers. Stream accesses are developed by MDC so the public can canoe, swim, camp, and fish. These accesses are very popular, especially on summer weekends. Mondays in the summer occupy my work team and I with cleaning up the accesses. On this Monday, my work team was either taking annual leave or on a western fire detail. It did not happen very often but today I was on my own. My first stop was Rippee Access because it gets the most use. This access lies at the junction of Rippee and Bryant Creeks. A highlight of the area is the historical site of Native American camps and a Civil War skirmish. As I pulled into the area, I noticed there were still several families camping and all of the trash barrels were full. I drove to the first barrel and it was overflowing with trash. There was a family fishing nearby obviously amused by my task at hand. (I think they may have known something I did not.) I tried to pull the heavy duty, large garbage bag and found it too heavy to pull out. I had never had this happen before and wondered what was in the bottom of that barrel? My plan was to tie the top of the trash bag and lay the barrel down on the ground, so I did not have to fight gravity. I still could not get it out. I noticed even more people watching me, but no one offered to help. I sat down in front of the barrel and placed a boot on each side of the barrel. I grabbed the top of the bag and pulled it, while pushing the barrel away from me with my legs. I did not know that there was a hole in the metal barrel which created a sharp edge that cut the side of the bag. I ended up on my back and had 15 pounds of rotten pork and beans in my lap. (So rotten the raccoons had not bothered with this trash can.) I know it was 15 pounds because the container that came out empty was clearly labeled. As I laid there contemplating my next move, one of the fishermen walked up and said, "I do not know how much they pay you, but I know it is not enough." He then walked away and resumed fishing. I got up, took off my boots and jumped into the creek. After rinsing off the beans, I grabbed a shovel and some empty trash bags and cleaned up the mess. Fortunately, the rest of the day was uneventful.

All our accesses have pit toilets. They are a small concrete building that sit on top of a concrete pit. These pits need cleaning out periodically. There are contractors that bring in pumping equipment, pump the privies clean, and haul the refuse to an approved sewage lagoon. We would bid these jobs out annually. One year we had a bid substantially lower than the others. The bid came from a father and son contractor and their bid was $50 per privy. Normally the bid is $200 to $300 per privy. One summer day, I was in the office and the phone rang. It was from a frantic lady on her cell phone. She said "You are not going to believe this, there is a man down in the privy at Rippee and he is cleaning it out with a bucket and passing it up to another man that is dumping it in his truck." Before I could leave the office, she called back and said they are dumping the waste from their truck onto MDC land. There you go, you get what you pay for. I fired that contractor and hired the $300 bid.

I enjoyed working with the landowners and the variety of personalities. Once I was in the office working on paperwork when two men walked in. One of them was a little over 5 feet tall and maybe 100 pounds. The other "gentleman" was 6 feet 6 inches and weighed close to 300 pounds without an ounce of fat.

It did not help he wore a skintight shirt accentuating his muscular assets.

The little guy started the talking with introductions. He told me his name and then asked if I knew his partner. When I shook my head no, the little guy asked if I ever watched TV on Saturday mornings? I said, "No, that is usually my time to do chores around the house." He introduced his partner as, "Professional Wrestler Ole Anderson." My first thought was big deal, no one knows professional wrestling, and it is all fake anyway, but I kept my thoughts to myself for obvious reasons, he was big! Ole said that he was a sawmill owner in Minnesota and the cost of electricity was too expensive and he was looking for a more affordable location to move his mill to. We did some more talking and then I suggested that we get into the truck and go look at a sawmill and the forest resource. We went to the closest sawmill about 5 miles north of town.

We arrived and got out of the truck. As I looked around for the sawmill owner, the sawmill workers stopped what they were doing and surrounded Ole, requesting autographs. I was completely surprised, and the sawmill owner was not very happy. After everyone got their autograph they went back to work. The sawmill owner listened and answered as Ole asked feasible questions for about 30 minutes. We drove off to look at some managed and unmanaged timber sites.

After walking in the woods for two hours, Ole said he was hungry and would buy lunch. We drove back to Ava and walked into a noon lunch crowd at Sue's Café. A hush fell over the crowd as we walked to the only open table. As soon as we sat down, people started coming over, wanting autographs. Again, I was astonished. We eventually finished eating and went back to the office. The two men thanked me for my time and drove off to see some more forest land on their own. I never saw or heard from then again. Well, that is not exactly true. I did turn on the TV Saturday morning and told the kids, "I know that guy!"

I got a phone call from a forest landowner that was requesting a timber sale. I got directions to his property and told him I would look at it. I went to his forested property and found a good stand of timber. The trees were in the 14 to 16-inch diameter class. This is determined by measuring the circumference of a tree at chest height and convert that to tree diameter (volume tables are in diameter). Fortunately, we have measuring sticks and measuring tapes that do the conversion for us. The forest products that are obtained from 14-inch diameter trees are of less value than 16-inch diameter trees. If the landowner waits about 10 years his trees will be 16 and 18 inches in diameter and more than double in value.

I wrote up all my findings and put it into a management plan which I mailed to him. About a month later an old man and his great grandson/driver entered my office. The old man was carrying the management plan in his hand. He dropped the plan on the desk and said, "I am 97 years-old and you are asking me to wait 10 years?" I explained my rationale for what I had written and that I did not have prior knowledge of his age. We talked a lot about forestry. As a youngster, he cut down Douglas Fir trees in Oregon with a crosscut saw. He helped build a railway across the country and he herded cattle on horseback from Colorado to Texas. He was an amazing man to talk to and his brain was sharp. He said he took no medication except for an aspirin every day.

Considering the situation, I said that I could conduct a managed timber sale on his property. The old man gave it some thought and said, "I will wait for a while." Five years went by and at the age of 102 he came walking back in with his great grandson and said, "I am ready for that timber sale." The work team and I marked the trees to take, leaving some good young ones to grow some more. We sent out bids to loggers and prepared a timber sale contract to protect the landowner. When the bids were opened the old man accepted the high bid and we monitored the cutting. All went well and both parties were happy. That was the last time that I saw that landowner even though he lived to be 107.

I received a call from the Jefferson City Central MDC Office, and they asked me to visit with a landowner in Taney County. His name was David Lewis and he wanted to discuss donating property to the agency. I made the call and set up a meeting on his property.

I called him and he was a pleasant, older man excited to hear that we were interested in acquiring his property. Mr. Lewis and his family had owned the property for over 90 years and with recent health issues he wanted someone to own the property after his death, someone that would not commercially develop it. (He knew this would happen with the property's proximity to Branson.) The Missouri Department of Conservation occasionally receives calls like this, but they do not always work out. Sometimes the landowner puts unreasonable limitations and restrictions on the property.

On the agreed upon day, I pulled into David Lewis' property and parked in the gravel driveway, behind an old pickup truck. Dave greeted me at the door with a warm welcome and invited me into his modest single level, farmhouse. He showed me into his kitchen and poured me a cup of coffee. Dave was a tall, thin, man with a warm pleasant smile. A very unassuming, simple man, that I would have never expected to be a millionaire if I had not already known it.

Mr. Lewis proceeded to tell me his story. His parents built a small house and farmed the land during the depression. David was an only child and grew up on the 362 acre farm. He would go to work at Sears Department Store but continued to live and work on the farm. He apparently saved every penny of his paycheck as he was a multimillionaire. He said that he had made some good investments!! He would later build the modest home where we sat.

He desired to give the property to the Missouri Department of Conservation, to be managed for wildlife and public use such as hiking trails, hunting and fishing. The land was near a lake resort and Mr. Lewis thought this was the best plan to keep the property from being commercially developed. The only other request was to name the area after the Lewis family.

He also planned to give a million dollars to each of three local Universities to be used as general scholarships for local students. I sat there in awe of this benevolent plan and honored to have a part in his last wishes!

The next step was to look at the property. All 362 acres were inspected via his old 4-wheel drive truck. The property was a mix of open pasture and scattered oak, hickory, and black walnut. We saw both deer and turkey as we drove around. The crown jewel of the property was a clear, spring-fed, Ozark stream, alive with Small Mouth Bass.

As we drove back to the house, he said there were only two issues. The cows that we saw in the pasture belong to his neighbor, Joe. Joe's grazing lease expired in 13 months and the expiration date would be our possession date. The other requirement was that he (Mr. Lewis) would be able to live in his house for the rest of his life and retain 5 acres adjoining the house to keep his horse on. I told him that I would include that in my report to

Headquarters, but I did not personally see any issues with those requests.

MDC accepted the donation and the terms. Over the next several months, MDC made many trips to the property to develop a resource management plan that focused on wildlife habitat improvement, parking areas, and hiking trail locations. Plans were also made to plant more trees along the creek bank to control stream bank erosion.

On one such trip to the Lewis tract, I met a neighbor that was curious about what was going on. I explained it and he got very excited about the chance to deer hunt on the future MDC property. I gave him my business card and requested he contact me with any ideas he might have.

We were one month away from owning the new property and my office phone rang and it was the neighbor I had given the business card to. He said there was logging equipment on the west side of the Lewis property and they have a large deck of Walnut logs stacked at the west gate. Mr. Lewis's house was on the east side and he could not see what was going on. I called the Sheriff and Greg, the local MDC forester, then jumped in my truck and headed that way.

When I arrived, the Sheriff was talking to the logger, who as it turns out was also a victim. Joe, the man that had been using the land for grazing, misrepresented himself as the landowner and hired the logger to harvest all the mature Black Walnut trees. These trees can be the most valuable tree in Missouri if they are straight, large diameter and without defect. Joe had collected $30,000 from the logger. The Sheriff immediately returned the logs to Mr. Lewis' property and gave back the logger his $30,000. The Sheriff then turned to me and asked if we needed anything else from him. I told him that the property was to belong to

MDC next month. I also stated that this likely will go to court to recover damages, so we might need him for a witness. He gave me his business card and drove off.

I went to Mr. Lewis' home and explained what happened. He was very upset as he had allowed Joe free grazing for years. Mr. Lewis said he had a lawyer that was working on his estate and would ask him for advice.

A month went by and the big day finally came when the property now belonged to MDC. The first order of business was to clean up the logging mess. I took pictures of the mess. I joined Greg and his work team as we piled all the cut tree tops so the wildlife could use them for shelter and nesting. We estimated the volume of the cut logs and contacted a logger to come out and give me a bid for the walnut trees. We sold him the logs and gave the money to Mr. Lewis.

The grass on the property was all fescue which has no nutritional value for wildlife. We planted some wildlife friendly grasses. Trees were planted along the stream for bank stabilization. This was necessary because the walnut trees were removed from the stream bank. Trees on a stream bank slow the water down during floods, thus reducing the energy of the water and slowing soil erosion. Shortly thereafter, we opened the property up to the public and fishermen began coming right away.

I received a phone call from a Springfield, Missouri lawyer named Jerry. He was Mr. Lewis' lawyer. He wanted to use me as an expert witness. I had never been referred to as an expert, but it sounded pretty good. The first meeting between the two sides was basically a pissing contest, and muscle flexing. The lawyers were talking about damages ranging from $30,000 to $60,000. When I got back to my office, an idea occurred to me. They were just talking about the removing of the walnut trees. But what about the stream bank erosion, and decreased wildlife habitat, and over-all aesthetics, as well as manpower to clean all this up?

A nationwide, certified tree company had designed a program that could generate dollar amounts for measuring the value of natural resources. For example, it considered the values of shade, trees both large and small, tree species, wind breaks, streams, wildlife, acreage, and vegetation. I entered all the factors into the program, and it produced a value of $350,000 that was lost by the unmanaged tree cutting.

I explained the whole thing to Jerry and could hear him smil-ing over the phone. At the next appointed meeting, I presented the program to the other side and they asked to close the meeting and set a date for the next one. The next meeting never arrived for me as they came to an agreement that favored Mr. Lewis' Estate! Mr. Lewis has since died but his legacy lives on.

Not everyone loves or even likes the Missouri Department of Conservation. Hunting laws are established to protect wild-life and maintain healthy populations. Too many deer and the farmers complain about deer eating their cattle pasture. Too few deer and you remove a food source and wildlife viewing from the public. Wildlife numbers are monitored by all MDC employees to stay on top of population changes.

The same goes for the forest resource. Too much cutting or too little cutting, and the resource is threatened. You have heard the saying, "you can't see the forest because of the trees". An unmanaged forest may look good from the road, but it may only have inferior species due to wildfire, insects and disease, or indis-criminate cutting.

The Missouri Department of Conservation conducts a peri-odic drain survey to see how much of the forest resource is being 'drained' (harvested) via logging. Every sawmill in the state is periodically surveyed to determine if the harvest rate is sustainable for the resource.

I had been conducting this standardized survey and all was going well. It is a good opportunity for the forester and sawmill owner to voice successes and concerns. I had only one more survey to complete and it was the worst. This mill owner (I will call him Butch to protect the innocent) was a mean man and a big man. He once put two men in the hospital with just his fists. He was arrested for getting mad at a school superintendent and threatening to kill him during a face to face discussion. Can you understand why I saved him for last on the survey?

I went to his sawmill and he had already shut down for the day. The deadline to get the survey done was the next day so I decided to see if he was home. I drove to his house and his pickup truck was in the driveway. Armed with my clipboard I knocked on his door. Butch opened the door and said, "What do you want?" I explained the survey and he opened the door and waved me in. I was feeling better but not for long. As I walked into the house, he motioned me to his couch. As I sat down, he closed the door and pulled a chair in front of the door and sat down. He said, "I am not going to answer any of your questions, but you are going to listen to me."

He was basically just mad at the world and proceeded to tell me. Butch did not like MDC because when we sent out bids for timber sales, we sent some to mills outside the county. He did not like MDC and never would (antigovernment). He continued to air his displeasures to me, and I got a question or comment in occasionally. Little did he know, I was getting answers to my survey and just stored them in my head. After listening to him for 30 minutes, he stood up, moved the chair from the door and said, "get out and don' come back unless you do everything I told you to do." I quickly exited before he thought of something else, and as soon as I got out of site, I pulled off the road and filled out the survey. That is what I call verbal judo.

The Missouri Department of Conservation was very good at providing training to do our jobs better. Everyone was required to take first aid and subsequent refreshers. All classes were hands on and we used the practice dummies and each other to become competent. I graduated from first aid school and was presented a certificate suitable for framing and headed for the house. I walked through the door and looked for someone to show off my certificate. No one was home. Within minutes my son ran into the house and told me Sharon (my next-door neighbor) "got thrown from her horse and she thinks she broke her arm!" I thought; 'This is not really happening.' My son did not appreciate my thought process and urged me to get moving. I grabbed an ace bandage and a phone book for a splint and took off running toward the neighbor. I saw her sitting up in her pasture and thought, good she is conscious! As I got near her, she sized up the items in my hands and said, "DON'T YOU FU**ING TOUCH ME!!" I was thinking, "They did not teach this in class." An ambulance arrived and they did basically what I was going to do. Obviously, my confidence was shaken, just because they had sexier equipment.

Fast forward two years. I had completed two more safety refreshers and my confidence had improved. I was in church and it was nearing the end of the service. The preacher asked me to close the service with prayer. As I was praying, the elderly lady standing beside me slumped to the floor. I quickly said, "Amen," followed by, "I need some help over here." I felt for a pulse and could not find one. I truly thought she was dead. From across the room came a fireman who felt for a pulse and then gently slapped her face. She immediately woke up and all was good. From then on, my prayers were much shorter.

I cherished my time in Ava, Missouri, working as their Resource Forester. I learned so much, met many great friends, and added again to my small family, with my last-born son. But in life all good things must come to an end. I accepted a promotion as Regional Forester and my office would now be in Springfield, Missouri. With this promotion my attention would now be focused more on administrative duties that don't necessarily make for great reading. However, a specifically fun part of this career starts now: Smokey the Bear!

PART 2

Smokey the Bear

Only you can prevent forest fires.

– Smokey the Bear

*With a Ranger's hat and shovel, and a pair of
dungarees you can find him in the forest always
sniffing at the breeze. People stop and pay
attention when he tells them to be aware because
everybody knows he is the fire prevention bear.
Smokey the Bear, Smokey the Bear, howling and
a-prowling and a-sniffing the air, he can find the
fire before it starts to flame. That's why they call
him Smokey, that's how he got his name.*

– Smokey's Ballad by Eddy Arnold (1952)

In the early years of wildfires, the US Forest Service developed an advertising campaign for fire prevention. I have never grown tired of the campaign which was known as Smokey the Bear. The idea was born when a little bear cub was rescued from a wildfire. This little cub became the image used to launch the fire prevention campaign on August 9, 1944. This campaign has grown immensely in popularity since. What a success story! Smokey became the third most recognized icon in the world behind Jesus Christ and Santa Claus. The US Forest Service primarily used television and radio advertising to get the fire prevention message all over the US.

As the popularity of Smokey grew, local fire agencies would have their fire fighters wear a Smokey the Bear suit and visit the children at schools and attend special events. This was often combined with a fire prevention movie and pamphlets for those in attendance. Back in the 1940's motion pictures were rare in rural areas and large crowds would come just to see the fire prevention movie and the people grew to love Smokey. In my early career (1980's) Smokey could talk to the kids. He would often give a brief reminder not to play with matches or teach about the stop-drop-and roll method if you found yourself on fire. I was working in Alton, MO and one of my "new" employees was petitioned with the job of wearing the Smokey suit. It was standard operating procedure that an MDC employee always accompany Smokey and on this occasion that escort was me. The new employee was extremely nervous, and I assured him how fun and easy this part of the job was and for him not to worry. We role played as to what exactly he was to share and today that would be the message of not playing with matches. We were presenting to third graders. The children enjoyed the fire prevention movie and now they were excited for the main attraction, Smokey the Bear.

The teacher of this class had done her research on Smokey and had previously presented many facts concerning Smokey and his history. When Smokey entered the room, he greeted the students and immediately hands went up to ask questions. The students were eager to satisfy their inquisitive minds.

Student #1: "Where were you born?"

Smokey (long pause): "In a cave."

Student #1: "Wrong, it was in New Mexico."

Smokey: "Yes, you are correct, that was where the cave was located."

Student #2: "How old are you?"

Smokey: I am 21. (The actual age of the employee in the suit, not Smokey.)

Student #2 "Nope, our teacher said you are 34."

Smokey: "21 in bear years."

At this point I am in awe of Smokey, he is quick.

Student #3 "What do little brown cub bears eat?"

Smokey: (Long pause) "Smart-alecky third graders!"

You could have heard a pin drop; the silence was golden. The question/answer time was over, and we exited the classroom without delay. This was the new employee's last Smokey Presentation. As an annual program for third grade students Smokey the Bear did not field any more questions – the bear was not allowed to talk. The assisting employee would introduce Smokey and allow them to come and shake his hand.

One particular year we had a very rural area that was experiencing a rather large number of wildfires. Strategically we decided to do a program in that area. A part of that program was talking to the third-grade class, showing them a video (True Story of Smokey the Bear) and having a question and answer period. When the movie was over, I began by asking the kids if any of them had ever seen a wildfire. Every single student in that class-room raised their hand. I then asked them, "How do these fires get started?" Immediately a little girl in the front row threw up her hand wildly in the air. Out of the corner of my eye I noticed the teacher shaking and lowering her head in fear of what was about to happen. I pointed to the enthusiastic young lady. With no hesitation she said, "Well sometimes all the men at my house get drunk and go set fires." Out of the mouths of babes! We did follow up on the "lead," and asked enough questions around the area that the fires stopped.

In 2007 the Springfield, Missouri area was hit with a destructive ice storm. Not only were homes damaged but so were the surrounding forests. Practically every mature tree in the forest had the tops broken off and laying on the forest floor. These dead branches could become fuel for wildfires for many years to come.

We contacted a US Forest Service Fire Prevention Team to help us out. The team toured the area to see the wildfire potential. Based on what they saw, they created a 2-year action plan to get the word out to the public. The plan included television commercials, door hangers, community meetings and interviews with the local news channels. They had another great idea that really interested me. Springfield is the home of the St. Louis Cardinals minor league team. One of the finest minor league baseball parks in the country is in Springfield. I am an avid baseball fan, so they had my attention. But first, we had to sell it to the General Manager of the Springfield Cardinals. The presentation was followed by an in-depth tour of the facilities, introductions to staff and players, with a stop on the field and training grounds. For a baseball lover, this was a dream come true. The idea we pitched (pun intended) was enthusiastically accepted and the Cardinals used this marketing campaign for several games that season. The

Cardinals evolved into one of MDC's best advertisers. Our plan included a large fire prevention display board in center field, fire prevention flyers to hand out to the fans as they left the stadium, and I saved the best for last, Smokey the Bear would throw out the ceremonial first pitch! After the first pitch, Smokey the Bear and his escort will walk around the stadium for photo opportunities and autograph Smokey baseballs. Because of my love of baseball, Smokey, AND my position as Regional Forester, I selfishly volunteered to dress the part of Smokey!

I practiced pitching to my son in the backyard while wearing the Smokey suit. Thankfully, we had a privacy fence to keep from scaring the neighbors. It was a sight to behold. I am glad I practiced as it was harder than I expected. Smokey's eyes were very small and if you moved your head, you could not see the catcher and the ball was likely to go anywhere. Game day arrived. The Springfield Cardinals were playing the St. Louis Cardinals in an exhibition game. I warmed up in the bull pen to the delight of the fans. Smokey was very nervous. I received an ovation as I was walking to the mound. I was waving excitedly, proving that a big bear can be a big ham.

Studying the mound, now my attention turned to my assigned task. The objective was to get the ball to the catcher in the air, it does not have to be a strike (but that would be nice if it was). I had to locate the catcher. I couldn't move my head because my eyes are too small. There were at least 25,000 people watching me as I tried to locate the catcher, and then not move my head. I was thinking about it too much! So here it goes, the wind up and the pitch. It was a ball, high, but catchable. I was relieved and happy! The catcher came out to the mound and gave me the ball. Smokey waved to his new adoring fans and strutted off to the home-team dugout.

The Fire Prevention Campaign was a success. We had no large wildfires for several years. Just for the record, I threw two more ceremonial first pitches. I ended up with one ball and two strikes!

Remember–Only **YOU** can **PREVENT FOREST FIRES!**

This Photo by Unknown Author is licensed under CC BY-SA

PART 3

WILDLIFE

'We reached the old wolf in time to watch a fierce
green fire dying in her eyes. I realized then, and
have known ever since, that there was something
new to me in those eyes – something known only
to her and to the mountain. I was young then,
and full of trigger-itch; I thought that because
fewer wolves meant more deer, that no wolves
would mean hunters' paradise. But after seeing the
green fire die, I sensed that neither the wolf nor
the mountain agreed with such a view.'

– Aldo Leopold

When Birds Run

I was driving my state pickup truck south on 5 Highway on my way to look at some privately-owned timberland. This highway offers a wonderful view of open grasslands and oak hickory forest. I glanced in my rear-view mirror and saw a UPS truck flashing his lights at me. I recognized the driver, Jim, and gave him a big wave. He continued to flash his lights at me, so I pulled over onto the shoulder of the road. Jim got out carrying a box like all good UPS guys do. The difference here was that the box had what looked like a dead Red Tail Hawk. Upon closer look, I noticed it was breathing but not conscious. Jim said the bird had flown into the side of his truck. Jim opened up my passenger door and put the bird on my passenger side floorboard. I waited until Jim drove off because my plan was to just lay the hawk in the grass beside the road. I shook the box and he did not move but I could still tell he was breathing, so I decided I would take him to the woods as I was almost there (I know what you are thinking, just wait till the end). I drove to the woods and parked on a trail in the shade. I rolled down all the windows because it was hot outside. I looked over at the hawk and he was still laying in the box. I got out of the truck and walked over to the passenger side and opened the door. To my surprise the bird leaped across and perched on the driver's door. He looked back at me and seemed to smile while defecating all over my door and cloth driver seats. This no longer is a mission of mercy as I am consumed with blind rage. I ran to the other side of the truck and the dirty bird jumped down and took off running through the timber. Who knew a hawk could run, and worse than that, could outrun me? I never caught up with him and he got the last laugh as the stain never came out of my truck upholstery.

OTTERS IN MISSOURI

Missouri had a healthy population of otters prior to human settlement but disappeared soon thereafter. MDC developed a plan to bring back the Otters to Missouri. There is a common transaction between states for acquisition of animals that are decreasing. In this scenario MDC traded turkeys to Alabama in exchange for river otters.

Previous otters received from Alabama were initially taken to a large warehouse near Columbia, Missouri. Danny and I were asked to go there and pick up 20 otters to be released in southern Missouri. We left early in the morning in a pickup that had a camper shell on the back. We arrived mid-morning at the warehouse and were introduced to a large room full of otters. I immediately was introduced to all the otters as they sounded their warning noise because of our entrance. In unison, the otters started screaming like a tom cat. I cannot put into words how loud and scary they sounded. A Wildlife Biologist brought in a carved-up roadkill deer carcass and began feeding the noisy critters. It was brutal to watch them eat, and it was easily evident that they were truly carnivores. Danny and I loaded ten cages into the pickup. Each cage had one male and one female in it. We started our trip back toward Douglas County's Rippee Creek for our first release. About halfway there we decided to stop for a bathroom break and something to drink. Danny was driving and I noticed an ornery smile came across his face. He parked the truck in front of the convenience store front door and then proceeded to open the camper shell by the hatch. I thought he was just giving then some fresh air.

We were standing just inside the front door drinking a soda and talking with an employee when the first customer walked by the open camper shell and those otters started their death scream. The poor man nearly fell from fright. Despite that scare, he joined the group to watch the next person to jump for fright. This went on for a few minutes and we decided that we better get down the road.

We pulled into the Rippee Creek parking lot and there was a large crowd that showed up for the release. The crowd included school kids, the local newspaper, MDC helpers, and curious adults. The MDC personnel started unloading five of the cages, ten otters in total. They put on quite a show for the people. You could almost see the smile on the faces of the otters as they played and swam upon release. I was carrying a cage down to the water's edge when my left foot slid in the mud and my right hand went into the wire cage. Immediately a male otter bit down on my middle finger. It felt like my finger had been smashed by a hammer. When I recoiled the otter hung on and I was suspending 35 pounds of otter by one finger. Fortunately, the otter turned loose and not too many people saw the incident. The other good thing, I was wearing a leather glove which was covered in blood. I walked around behind my truck so no one would see the carnage and by chance a doctor was present and followed me. I took the glove off and discovered the blood had come from the otter as he

47

was biting the cage trying to get out. I just had a smashed finger and eventually lost my fingernail. We took the remaining otters to the North Fork of the White River and released them without any fanfare or issues. Releases like these occurred throughout the state. Once again, the otter is a resident of Missouri.

BLACK BEAR IN MISSOURI

When the first surveyors came to Missouri in the 1800's, they made notes of the landscape and the animals present and included it all in their survey notes. These notes have been preserved and serve as a record of what Missouri looked like back then. Black bear was commonly mentioned in these notes. However, over the years black bear became almost extinct in Missouri. On the other hand neighboring state, Arkansas, had a healthy population of black bear for many years and in the early 2000's bear sightings were occurring more often in Southern Missouri as some of the young black bears made their way north. One young bear travelled all the way to St. Louis. When we started getting calls about seeing bear cubs, we knew that we had gone from a transient population to a breeding population. Black bears typically have one or two cubs per year which means the population can more than double annually.

Our first order of business was to determine how many bears were in Missouri and figure out how many bears southern Missouri could sustain without bear-to-human conflict. The Wildlife Division sought help from other states and developed a plan to trap bear, determine age, attach tracking devices, and take a blood sample for DNA purposes. The bears were trapped in two ways. A barrel trap was used the most because bears associate trash barrels with food. The bear would smell the bait in the end of a barrel which was laying on its side. As the bear crawls in he/she bumps a trigger, and a vented door drops over the opening. The other trap used was a leg hold trap. The bear goes to the bait on the ground and steps on the trigger of a leg hold trap. All traps were checked daily by MDC employees. The primary bait used was day old donuts. The trapping had to take place before the acorns fell from the oak trees in the fall because the bears would rather have acorns than donuts.

I received a call at my office that they had a large bear trapped and needed help. It was only about 15 miles from my office. I arrived at the trap site and I saw my first Missouri bear! The tag on the bear indicated he had been trapped three times, all within a 30-mile radius. He was given a shot that allowed him to be conscious, but he could not move.

He was huge, weighing in at 485 pounds (the largest captured bear was 492 pounds). To weigh the bear, it was tied to a pole, which was attached to scales that were attached to another pole that we lifted. It took six men to lift the bear from the ground. It was scary working around a bear that had his eyes open and constantly licking his lips. Because he had been caught before, we did not have much to do except wait for the drug to wear off. After about an hour, he stood up, looked around and walked off looking for donuts.

Photo Credit: Brad Jump

In order to tag the bear, we had to give her
tranquilizers to achieve the task.
Photo Credit: Brad Jump

PART 4

Prescribed Fire

*'One of the penalties of an ecological education
is that one lives alone in a world of wounds.
Much of the damage inflicted on land is quite
invisible to laymen. An ecologist must either
harden his shell and make believe that the
consequences
of science are none of his business, or he must be
the doctor who sees the marks of death in a
community that believes itself well and does not
want to be told otherwise.'*

- Aldo Leopold

Prescribed Fire is an important management tool used throughout the United States. It is well planned out ahead of time for a specific management purpose. There are many components of a properly managed prescribed fire.

The objectives will vary around the country due to different landscapes and vegetation. Some objectives include:

Wildland Fuel Management: Reducing heavy wildfire fuels under conditions where escape is not likely. Heavy fuels may accumulate due to bug killed trees and dead or dormant vegetation.

Wildlife Habitat Improvement: Warm season native grasses are present in many states. These grasses can grow as tall as six feet providing food and cover for wildlife. When they go dormant, they fall to the ground forming a dead blanket of grass that smothers the next crop of grass. Prescribed fire removes the dead grass.

Eastern Red Cedar: Especially invasive, Eastern Red Cedar can take over an abandoned pasture. It is a designated noxious weed in Oklahoma. To kill it with prescribed fire, you must burn the whole tree to kill it. If the fire does not burn to the top the tree will survive. Eastern red cedar can burn very volatile.

Other components of a prescribed burn include:

Burn Plan: A detailed plan written by the "burn boss" and reviewed by supervisors. The plan tells who, what, when, where and how. The plan describes how the burn needs to be carried out and what weather conditions are needed to achieve objectives. Other considerations are time of year, contingency plans, and smoke management. Also needed is the number of firefighters (we often use these opportunities to train new firefighters). The equipment that is needed to complete the burn safely is listed too. Where is the smoke going and how to reduce the impact of smoke on nearby communities?

Contacts: Anyone that may be impacted by the prescribed fire. This may include nearby residents, local fire departments, other agencies, and law enforcement.

Weather: A call is made to the National Weather Service and a request is made for a "spot weather forecast." By giving them the location of the prescribed fire, they provide a forecast for that specific location.

Briefing: A detailed briefing involves all personnel, making sure that everyone knows their objectives, assignments, the weather and radio frequencies.

Test Fire: A small test fire is set at the starting point to see if the fire behavior is what you expected. If it is then you continue with the prescribed burn. If not, the test fire is extinguished.

Missouri State University in Springfield afforded me the opportunity to teach after I retired. I taught Forest Management and Wildland Fire Management. Live fire training offered in the Wildland Fire Management class was enjoyable not only for the students but my favorite too. It was a "field trip," literally, toward the end of the semester. About 30 minutes from campus MDC owned a large parcel of land where we had set up a prescribed fire. The class was divided into two crews and given specific roles. They had to devise the burn plan and were provided tools that most had never handled or even seen before.

Photo Credit: Tim Stanton

It is rare to find wildlife harmed during a prescribed fire. Most critters run away due to all of the people, trucks and ATV activities. The initial burn is a backing fire that moves slowly, allowing the animals to escape.

We had just completed a prescribed fire in tall grass. My co-worker Greg and I were talking about the successful burn. I asked Greg if he was afraid of snakes, and he said, "usually not if I see them before they see me." The reason I asked was because a Copper Head Snake (poisonous) had slithered out of the burned grass and stopped between Greg's legs. I said look down, he instantly became an Olympic high jumper. Both Greg and the snake survived.

On another project, we had just completed a prescribed fire that had both grass and trees. The fire burned hotter than we had planned, but none of the fire jumped over our control lines. There were three young men that were on their first prescribed fire. I explained to them that it was time to do mop up by patrolling the entire control line to make sure that the entire fire was completely out. I told them that they needed to look up into the treetops because a fire that burns hot can send enough heat to the treetops to catch them on fire. I no more finished my sentence when a burning branch fell out of the tree we were standing under and landed between us. The rookies looked up at the top of the tree, looked at the burning branch on the ground and then at me like I was a fire prophet. I never said anything to them, but I was just as surprised as they were.

After I retired from MDC, I subcontracted with an Oklahoma based Company named Chloeta (pronounced Show-Lay-Ta). This Native American-based contractor provides wildland fire crews and engine crews where needed.

Chloeta had a long-term contract with the military at Fort Chafee Military Base near Fort Smith, Arkansas. This Facility was home to the Navy Seals and the Air Force, A-10 Wart Hog aircraft.

This base was also known as the basic training facility that trained Elvis Presley. It is an interesting place to do prescribed fire in tall grass. On the ground lay live ammunition dropped by soldiers and the razor sharp casentino wire. The bullets were not a big threat. A bullet that explodes outside a gun is like fireworks. If you do not have your fingers or face in the wrong place you are okay. The sharp razor wire was no fun. If you got into it, help was required to get out. The rule was, if you did not drop it, do not pick it up. I did find some land mines lying on top of the ground that Range Control knew nothing about.

The Wart Hog's Aircraft would fly very close to the ground as they practiced bombing with live bombs on a destroyed piece of landscape named Potato Hill. They also fired a 50-caliber gun that made more noise than the bomb. When possible, they used our prescribed fire smoke to fly through in route to the practice bombing.

On one occasion we were on the east side of the facility conducting a large prescribed burn. We heard and felt a large explosion. A visible plume of smoke came up and it appeared to be at the Seal's restricted training area. About ten minutes went by and we received a radio call from Range Control asking us to respond to the wildfire. My co-worker Mark and I went over to scout it out. We entered the Seal's training area just as they were coming out.

The point of the fire origin was very easy to find. There was a crater big enough to hide a Volkswagen. The wildfire ran up the grass and brush hill fast and was around 30 acres already. The logistics for us was complicated because we could not abandon the prescribed fire for fear of it becoming a wildfire. We put ten guys including me on the wildfire and left ten guys on the prescribed fire. We worked well into the night on both fires. When it was all said and done, the wildfire was contained at 360 acres while the prescribed fire stayed within its control lines at 240 acres.

Mark and I were summing it all up afterwards and I suggested a new tee shirt that would read, "When the SEALS RUN OUT CHLOETA RUNS IN!" We had a good laugh, but it was all in jest as we have nothing but respect for them. We were in the right place at the right time and glad to help.

I assisted the US Park Service as a safety officer, on a prescribed fire at Wilson's Creek National Battlefield near Springfield, Missouri. This National Park was the site of a large Civil War battle that claimed 2,300 lives. The soldiers that died were all buried on the site and then later exhumed and buried at Arlington National Cemetery (this will be a significant part of this story).

The U.S. Park Service maintains this National Park as close as possible as it was during the Civil War. There are original buildings on site and tall native prairie grass vegetation that needs to be burned every five years to maintain it.

We had a 20-person crew and a five-person burn module to do the prescribed fire. A burn module consists of highly trained prescribed fire personnel and they have a trailer full of equipment specific to prescribed fire. We started with a briefing that explained the objectives and assignments. Hazards were identified, mainly the historic buildings on site, nearby private homes, and volatile, tall grass fuels. The park was closed to the public for the day.

There is a black topped trail that circles the park. We used this as our fire break and set the prescribed fire on the inside of the trail. If the fire does not jump over the trail, then it will literally be a "walk in the park."

The plan was to use an ATV drip torch to lay down a continuous line of fire on the inside of the walking trail. A drip torch is filled with three parts diesel and one part gasoline in a metal container that when lit, drips fire from a nozzle. The 20-person crew will follow behind the drip torch to make sure the fire does not jump over the trail/control line.

All was going well. The ATV operator (Ron) came to a spot that the fire was not burning as hot as needed so he drove the ATV and torch into the grass, well away from the trail. Due to tall grass and hilly terrain, we lost sight of him.

Then came a call over the radio. I have fallen into an old grave; the ATV is on top of me. The torch is dripping fire. I was one of three that were first to arrive to his location. One guy started knocking the fire down as myself and the other firefighter got the ATV off Ron. I got the torch turned off. We were able to walk Ron out, shaken, and sore, but nothing serious. The thought of dying in someone else's grave sounded like a horror movie.

We were within 20 minutes of being finished and did so without any further problems. We gathered all fire personnel together and did an "after action review". This is where each person can respond to three questions: What was planned? What happened? And, What can we do better next time?

The consensus answered:

<u>What was planned:</u> A high-profile prescribed fire and contained the fire within the trail, and with no harm to any structures.

<u>What happened:</u> We carried out the burn as planned, without any fire escaping our control line. An incident occurred that could have been serious. An ATV fell in an empty grave and trapped the operator. The incident could have been catastrophic but fortunately the operator walked away.

<u>What can we do better next time:</u> Do a better job scouting the burn area looking for potential hazards. Don't operate an ATV in tall grass without a scout walking ahead of you. Most importantly, don't operate ATVs around open graves.

We had a prescribed burn scheduled for a piece of state land near Joplin, Missouri. I got this idea to make it a public education event. I contacted the Joplin television station and informed them of the burn and my motive for doing so.

The burn day arrived, and the weather forecast was ideal. I gathered my six co-workers to lay out my plan for the burn and for the press. I wanted all of them to talk with the media and explain our objectives and tactics.

The media arrived as we were about to begin. I invited them to talk with all the guys and learn as much as possible about prescribed fire. I gave them instructions on what to do if something went wrong and where their safe area would be.

Everyone on the burn crew took turns in front of the camera, explaining the tactics and objectives. At one point we had a good surprise. A fire whirl, also called a fire tornado, developed. On any fire these can be a substantial problem. They occur when the atmospheric pressure is very high. In this situation it was no more than a good photo opportunity. We finished the prescribed fire with no issues. The news lady said, "this will be on tonight's 7:00 news." We all gathered around the TV to watch. The news lady introduced the segment by saying, "this is a prescribed burn done on state land by MDC, south of Joplin. This is a fire tornado. We will be back with the sports." So much for education.

MISSOURI'S CHERNOBYL

Not far from Columbia, Missouri is a nuclear power plant that provides electricity to thousands of residents. The facility sits in an open grassy field that is several hundred acres. The grasslands are managed by the Missouri Department of Conservation.

A prescribed fire was planned for the native grasses on the facility's property with a goal to improve the quality of the native warm season grasses. These grasses need to be burned every three to five years to remove the old dead grass and enhance the new young grasses. Bobwhite quail chicks use this mix of open ground and grassy cover to find insects and seeds and have protection from predators.

Planning meetings were held for those participating in the burn. An important consideration was the wooden power poles that were on the property, taking electricity from the plant to the residents. Prior to the prescribed burn, all vegetation was removed from a 10-foot circle around each pole. The burn day arrived, and all participants gathered for a briefing. This required meeting gave everyone their specific responsibilities. All the weather factors (temperature, wind speed, wind direction, and humidity) were checked to make sure they were within compliance of the burn plan. Phone calls were made to the power plant and nearby fire departments so they knew the burn was about to begin. A test fire was set to make sure the fire behavior was as planned. The burn boss gave the order to begin the prescribed burn.

All was going as planned until...A lone eastern red cedar tree burst into flames. This is not a bad thing because they are very invasive. However, this tree sent a large black smoke cloud skyward into the above power line. There were carbon elements in the cloud that caused an electrical arc from the power line to the ground. This arc created an electrical short which shut down the nuclear power plant!!!

Under normal conditions, when shut down is needed at a nuclear plant, it is done slowly and systematically to allow everything to cool down. There was no cooling down this time. Now for the good news. When this facility was built, they planned for an inappropriate shut down. The engineers learned this from the Chernobyl incident in Russia. Everything worked as planned, avoiding a major incident. MDC shut down all prescribed fires statewide until we all could learn from this mishap.

PART 5

Wildfire

When we abuse land because we regard it as a commodity belonging to us. When we see land as a community to which we belong, we may begin to use it with love and respect.

– Aldo Leopold

FIRST FIRE - WORST FIRE

In 1985 I was ready to take a spot on an out west wild-land fire-fighting crew. I took my first qualifying tests to be a wild-land firefighter. One had to complete classroom training and pass the written exams in the S130 and S190 coursework. After successful completion of those tests you took the step test. This test consisted of stepping up and down on a 15-inch box for five minutes and then a proctor counted your heart rate. If your heart rate was past a designated threshold then you failed the endurance test and were not allowed to be dispatched. Later the endurance test was changed and is currently used today. The official name of the test is called the "Pack Test." The Pack Test was designed to burn the same number of calories as it takes to construct a containment line for 45 minutes. With this test, you must carry 45 pounds in a pack on your back for three miles and do it in less than 45 minutes. This test was a better measurement of endurance and upper body strength. Once all the required testing has been passed you are issued a red card and then allowed to be put "on the board" or on call for deployment. A firefighter's career most generally begins on the fire line. To achieve promotions a task book must be completed which is on the job training. My first wild-land fire experience consisted of a 20-person MDC crew. We had been directed by dispatch to have our fire gear packed and ready to go. Two days had gone by without a call. The call finally came in at 4:00 a.m. I was instructed to have myself and fire gear in Rolla, Missouri by 7:00 a.m. It was a two-hour drive for me so there was no time to waste. Once the team was there, we were briefed and headed to Oregon via a federal plane. We flew to Boise, Idaho and were transferred to school buses and then driven to Oregon. We arrived at the fire only to find that it had mostly been rained out while we were in route. Our crew was given two days of mop up with the temperatures in the 40's (90's back home in Missouri). The second night it rained, and everyone had a cold miserable night. Day three and four we broke down the fire camp and prepared to go home. Some would say that this was a completely wasted fire trip. Not at all! I had never been to Oregon.

The mountain vistas were beautiful, and I heard my first elk bugle. The sunrises and sunsets were incredible. Several of that 20-person crew never took another trip. In my mind there had to be more and I was ready to go again during the next season.

THE NEXT FIRE THE BEST FIRE

My second wild-land fire would take me to central California. The crews came together from all over the US and met at a California Forest Service's field office for staging. Many fires were on the loose and we were on standby as the operation team decided on which fire each individual/crew would deploy to. We were standing around talking about what we were going to spend our fire money on when a commotion kicked up to the left of us. The large group of fire fighters beside us began to part allowing a young lady to pass through. As she got closer, I could see she was extremely fit. Then she got close enough where I could read her tee shirt, "GET OUT OF MY WAY OR I WILL KICK YOUR ASS." Needless to say, no one challenged her. Back then and even today, females are rare on the fire line. "According to the most recent NFPA statistics, women represent 7.3 percent of all U.S. firefighters. And about 12 percent of the permanent wildfire suppression jobs at the Forest Service, Bureau of Land Management and National Park Service are occupied by females." https://www.frontlinewildfire.com/trailblazers-women-wildland-firefighting/

In my career on the fire-line I only worked with three women firefighters. Predominantly the careers for women that I witnessed included wild-land engine crews, hand crews, hot shot crews, GIS tents (Geographic Information System) and dispatching.

After waiting 24 hours in the California Forest Service's field office we were taken to the base camp which was near Yosemite National Park. A base camp is where all the administration tents, laundry, food, showers etc. are assembled that support multiple fires and crews. We were then helicoptered into a spike camp. The fire we were sent to was 500 acres, with a hot shot crew already in place. Everyone was supplied with Vietnam Era M.R.E.'s and 40 gallons of water for the entire crew. Two choices of MRE's were available: freeze-dried beef or pork. You had to pour water on what looked like a piece of brown Styrofoam to "soften" the brown slab they labeled as meat. Fortunately, a piece of sponge cake and some dried fruit accompanied the meal. There was a very large spring-fed stream nearby, but we were told not to drink from it, despite it being one of San Francisco's water supplies. As a firefighter we are always looking to quench our thirst and the temptation of this spring was sometimes more than we could bear.

Our first shift on the fire line was like none I would ever experience again in my life. We hiked to an opening in the Sugar Pine Forest. The trees were 150 to 200 feet tall; it was a sight to behold. The forester in me automatically began to figure that one sugar pine had as much board feet of lumber as 10 acres of Missouri oak. When one chooses a career, it is vital to have a passion for what you do. As I walked through the majestic pine, I felt it an honor that my training had brought me to this juncture in my career; to do my part in helping save the beautiful forests for all to enjoy. Our job was to build a containment line at a creek bed and continue building the line up a steep hill. Half of the crew went to the top of the hill alongside a hot shot crew, and they were building a fire break down toward us. We were making good progress when the wind began picking up from the direction of the fire. The fire was about 300 yards away, but it had climbed into the tops of the sugar pine. Embers were falling from the sky and starting spot fires outside of our constructed containment line. Frantically we tried to put the spot fires out but there were too many. I looked up the hill and saw the hot shots and the other half of our crew running down the hill toward us. Our crew supervisor yelled, "Follow them." You did not have to tell me twice! When we got to our designated safe zone which was in the creek bed, the first task was roll call, everyone was present. As I surveyed the situation, I noticed that all of us had small black holes in our Nomex shirts, meaning that there were many sparks flying. We lost all our containment line, so we retreated past the fire's location and started the process once again.

Forest fires generally have two or four flanks. Our crew was on the east flank and had successfully contained it. This fire had a total of four flanks. We still had some mop up to do. Mopping up is the term used to ensure that nothing "hot" is next to the containment line on the black side. To ensure that the mop-up was completed we needed to patrol the fire break, making sure that nothing jumped the containment line. As a young firefighter I learned that different regions had the same definitions but used different words for several fire terms – on this particular day, I learned the following:

Slop Over: Western States

Catch Out: Texas

Break Over: Missouri

All three of these words simply mean that the fire jumped the containment line. To accomplish the task at hand we broke into seven groups with each group having three firefighters. The groups spread out along the line. The crew boss could tell that each of us were fatigued. We had put in already a very long day of strenuous work in hot temperatures. Our crew boss instructed each group to allow one person from the group to take a little break/nap while the other two worked on the line. I was patrolling the line and noticed one of the firefighters had nodded off and his hardhat had fallen from his head and into a warming fire. The hard plastic helmet now had enough abnormalities that it looked like he had been to hell and back. We continued along the line and watched the sun rise. As the sun was coming up that was our cue to gather up and start the hike back to camp. Our containment line was considered a success since we did not have a slop-over. We had worked close to a 30-hour shift. We were all starving, stinky and sleepy! Each of us had been provided one of those horrible MRE's to eat and 40 gallons of water for the entire crew. As we arrived at camp, our replacement crew was walking out. They stepped aside as if to give respect to the walking dead. Our sooty faces, holey shirts and one melted hardhat made them wonder what they were marching in to.

The first order of business for all of us was to SLEEP! We got around 5-6 hours of sleep under the hot sun. Everyone was slow in getting up. Another Missouri crew member, Stan, came over to me and said, "Hey, come with me, I have something to show you." Keith, another guy from Missouri, was sleeping and was really snoring. While he was sound asleep black ants were going in and out of his mouth. Stan said, "A man shouldn't have to live like that," and then turned and walked away. You gotta be tired to not feel ants all over your mouth! We soon discovered that our crew was out of water. Normally, supplies are flown into spike camps by a helicopter, but there had been way too much wind and smoke for them to land. The crew boss asked my squad to go to the river and bring back water. This was the same river we were not supposed to drink from. The river was about two miles away from camp. While the walk was hot, the water was wet and cold. My squad of five members carried back five gallons of the water each. As we walked back into camp, we arrived just in time to see the supply helicopter lift off. The smoke had cleared enough to bring in supplies, including cases of canned water. The water was from a brewery and had a stale beer taste to it. No one complained about the taste of the beer water except for one guy who happened to turn 21 that day; to our surprise it was his first "beer."

The next day found us building a second containment line toward the river which was the west flank that we had gotten our water from. A small single engine airplane flew directly overhead. I asked out loud, "Was that a lead plane?" My question was immediately answered by an air tanker which dropped red fire retardant on us. What a sticky mess, which we learned also attracts flies. It was not quitting time so working in a sticky mess and surrounded by flies sure made for a LONG workday! We did however get the containment line to the creek and several crew members jumped in the cold water to wash off the dirt and fire retardant. San Francisco received a bad batch of water that day. When we got back to camp, we had two surprises. The first surprise: A new fire crew had moved into camp. They set their tents up in the area we had designated for our crew to defecate our digested MRE's. In this particular spike camp, there weren't any outhouses, so when one had to use the bathroom, they took off to the designated area with a shovel. After their bathroom duties were completed it was proper fire etiquette to cover over your droppings. Still to this day I am just not sure how this new fire crew couldn't smell our man-made port-a-potty!

The other surprise was a pack-mule train that brought us our FIRST hot meal in insulated canisters. We were all starving and especially for something other than an MRE. We opened the canisters and found Chicken Cordon Bleu. It was very tasty. However, four of our crew did get sick, either from food poisoning or from their body rejecting "real" food.

While on a short break later in the week the crew boss gave us a briefing on bear encounters. He said, "If you walk up on a bear just stand still and avoid eye contact." Johnny, a guy on the crew, just started laughing and said, "That is pretty funny, now what do we really do?" The Crew Boss said, "Seriously that's what you really do." There was a little bit of a pause and Johnny replied, "That's not for me, all I have to do is outrun the slowest guy."

Crews are usually limited to 14 days on the fire-line and it was time for us to go home. We had the satisfaction of knowing the fire was out and we had something to do with that. For many of the crew this was their first or second western fire. Several of the crew never deployed again for out west fire detail. For me, I enjoyed fighting fires so much I did it for another 40 years. When we boarded the plane for home, Richie was still wearing his melted hardhat!

Take-aways from this memorable fire:

A. If a hot shot crew is running to a safe zone, ask NO questions, just follow them

B. Invest in a GOOD pair of boots! During my career I had two pairs of Redwing boots and they were worth every dollar!

C. When you see a lead plane, learn what comes next; the fire-retardant plane that drops the chemical on whatever or whomever is in its path.

D. Look down at the ground (no eye contact) when meeting a bear, or be able to outrun the slowest guy.

WESTERN FIRE HIGHLIGHTS

Almost a movie star! I was part of a fire crew in Idaho and we were busy building a fire break when our crew boss received a call on the radio from the Division Supervisor that a fire had jumped over a containment line and they wanted our crew to get there ASAP. When a Division Supervisor calls and says come, you stop what you are doing and go! We grabbed our tools and took off running. We passed two crews on the way which made me wonder why those crews had not been asked since they were closer to the needed area. I justified it in my mind that we must be a better crew and kept on jogging. As we got close to the fire, I noticed four safety officers standing like statues overlooking the fire. We immediately began digging a dirt fire break around the wildfire. We worked about 15 minutes and the Division Supervisor said, "You all can stop now." We all looked up confused as the fire was not contained. We then saw three movie cameras recording our work. The fire was staged and could not go anywhere because it would stop at a road. The Division Supervisor told us that this was a Stephen Spielberg movie crew, and they were filming a movie named "Always" starring Richard Dryfus. I was a little upset at first since we had worked our tails off and someone could have been injured. I mellowed out when I thought about seeing our crew in a movie. However, they did not use any of our footage. Check it out, as it wasn't a bad movie, but in my opinion if they had used our footage, we would have made it better.

A RARE OPORTUNITY FOR A
MISSOURI BOY

Iwas a strike team leader on a fire in Glacier National Park, supervising five wild-land fire engines and the crew that accompanied the engines. We were protecting structures near McDonald Lake. The night shift came in to relieve us and all my personnel headed to the chow line. I chose to forego eating and take a scenic drive on the Highway to the Sun. Tourists are known to travel to this region for the sole purpose of driving this highway. Knowing that I might never have the opportunity again to see the ever-popular tourist spot, I took full advantage with the time afforded to me. Highway to the Sun runs alongside the National Park. Normally there are thousands of vehicles that travel this highway daily, however, due to the fire the highway was closed. Since I was a leader on the fire and had my own truck, I could take a drive. The fire was south and west of the highway. Since the road was closed the wildlife felt safe to graze alongside the highway instead of deep in the woods. It was basically a zoo without bars. There were many animals that I had never seen before. I did however spot a deer, big horned sheep, eagles and moose. The multiple colors of the plants and trees that had yet to be affected by the fire was a sight to behold. I am appreciative that I had a career where I was allowed some rare opportunities and it should serve as a life lesson for all, that when you love your job you never really work a single day of your life.

You Gotta Be Flexible on a Fire-line

While on the fire at Glacier National Park my job duty changed from a strike team leader on engines to being a task force leader of two 20-person crews. One has to be flexible while out west. Learning how to adapt to new surroundings is a key component in out west fires. One of the crews I was supervising was 100% Hispanic. The crew boss and two squad bosses spoke English. However, the other men on the crew only spoke Spanish. I had taken one year of Spanish in high school and my father was a buyer for a large corporation in which he spoke a good amount of Spanish. Having this under my belt I could communicate enough to get by but relied heavily on the crew and squad bosses to explain my commands to the team. One day I was scouting the fire and was standing in an opening in the middle of the forest.

The Hispanic crew came running out of the woods headed toward the transport trucks. They were screaming, "Oso grande." I had NO clue what Oso grande meant. One of the guys stopped – looked at me and said in English, "Big bear." My Red Wing Boots quickly fell in step with the crew to get the heck out of there! Grizzlies were common in this area and I was thankful to add a new phrase to my limited Spanish vocabulary!

OUTHOUSE NIGHMARE

The Missouri crew was huddled up in camp telling stories. My buddy, Keith, walked off to spend some time in the outhouse. Ross, another crew member, was waiting on Keith to come out for his turn. Keith exited and Ross entered and noticed a wallet lying on the outhouse floor. He opened it up and discovered it was Keith's. Ross exited the john and approached Stan saying, "I found Keith's wallet on the floor of the john." Stan gave his devilish grin and said, "Let's have some fun." Stan put the wallet in his pocket and walked back to the group and stood on the opposite side from Keith and then said loudly, "You are not going to believe what I just found. I walked into the outhouse and noticed there was a wallet laying in the s@&t. I buried that wallet with my own deposit." Instantly everyone began feeling their pockets! In a pitiful voice and having NO color left in his face, Keith said, "That had to be my wallet." Instead of pity, Keith received a unanimous belly laugh from the crew. Stan said nothing. Keith walked over to the supply desk and asked for two large trash bags. Keith slowly walked toward the outhouse. He had placed the trash bags over his arms in order to use them as gloves. He opened the door to the outhouse and stepped inside.

The entire crew was there to cheer him on. Just as Keith was about to dip his hands down into all that nasty output Stan hollered, "Hey Keith, here is your billfold." The group broke out yet again in hysterical laughter. Keith's initial expression was one of murder, but then a smile escaped and we all could sense a relief in Keith's demeanor. It was a learning experience for me as I now always check for my wallet when exiting an outhouse.

COYOTE

Fire suppression tactics are determined by many factors. These include burnable fuels, weather, number of personnel, terrain, accessibility, structures, cultural features and even politics. Coyote tactics are used when access to the fire is limited, such as lightening fires in rugged terrain. These tactics require firefighters to live and work on the fire line.

Coyote Tactics: "A progressive line construction duty involving self-sufficient crews which build fire-line until the end of the operational period, remain at or near the point while off duty, and begin building fire-line the next operational period where they left off" (Glossary nwcg.gov).

As the rotary-powered time machine took off, I realized I was in a different world. Perhaps in a place a non-Indian had never stepped foot. Our crew from Missouri was dropped off on top of a mountain ridge in Idaho. The sun was setting and introduced a full moon. The only sound was the breeze in the ponderosa pine. There were no traffic jams...stores...or people...just our crew embracing the beauty of the moment. The silence was loud, and I was indeed in a special place! To this day I have never witnessed a sunset such as this one... sitting on the edge of a canyon watching the sunset as if I were watching God's drive-in movie. There was no smoke, no haze, no air pollution, and no noise. Each of us mesmerized by the moment. Once the matinee was over, it was time to roll out the sleeping bag and sleep under the stars. As I lay awake the stars took that moment to show off. Even though I was looking at the same stars as I see in Missouri, these stars looked like giant marshmallows. We woke up to a beautiful sunrise, and it was time to go to work. With the coyote tactics, our assignment was going to be building a fire containment line on the ridge using hand tools and chainsaws. We did this for sixteen hours. A helicopter brought us drinking water. and some hot containers of food. After eating we pulled out the sleeping bags and fell asleep. The next morning a helicopter brought us a hot breakfast. This same game plan went on for eight days. We had multiple layers of dirt and a few blisters. We got a helicopter ride to camp and went straight to the showers. Our line stopped the fire's progress and we received an "atta boy" at the morning briefing.

HOT POTATO

I was sent to the west flank as a Division Supervisor. I was to tie in with the hot shot crew, work with them and get a feel for the terrain. A helicopter ride to my destination gave me a good look at the fire and the terrain. The crew boss met up with me and filled me in on the crews' progress. I took off on my own to assess the current plan. Despite the fire the view was beautiful. There were steep mountains in every direction. There were no homes in danger but there was a historic mining site to the north of the fire. I continued my hike, looking for any options to control this fire. My radio broke the silence of nature, telling that a dry lightning fire was coming in from the west. Within minutes lightening started hitting the ground all around me. When you are on top of a mountain, there is no place to go; they teach us to stay away from trees, squat down and stand on your toes, much like a baseball catcher. The storm moved off as fast as it came up after several close calls. I stood up and radioed in that I was okay.

I continued my hike looking for tactical options and noticed a new smoke coming up about a half mile to the west. I called back to the Incident Commander (IC) and told him about the new fire. If this new fire took off it would move toward the crew to the east. A helicopter was launched to go look at the new fire.

There were three fires. One was in a group of pine trees, about 17 acres, one fire was in steep canyon and the third fire was in an open field. A 20-person crew was dispatched to the fire on the trees. The other two fires were smoldering.

My orders for the next day were to scout out a location to construct an eastern control line that would contain the original fire. I checked the map and figured out some possible line locations for me investigate. Before I began my hike, I contacted the Look Out from the crew. I told him where I was going and asked him to let me know if the fire picked up. I took off on my hike and found a long rock scree running north and south. A rock scree is a rockslide made up of golf ball sized round rocks; it was about 20 feet wide and 1/2 mile long. The radio broke the silence and the Look Out said, "The fire behavior is picking up and you need to get to your safety zone." Earlier in the day, I had identified a safety zone. It was a wide spot in the rock scree that had a large boulder in the middle that could be used as a heat shield. It was tough going, all up hill in the round rocks. I made it to my safety zone about 15 minutes before the fire got to me. My safety zone was just the right size for one person and the big boulder worked well as a heat shield. I got some good fire pictures, up close and personal. The Incident Commander asked over the radio if I was okay. I replied that I had an MRE to eat and a front row seat of the show. It was several hours before the fire cooled down enough to walk out. Later I was humbled to hear that a fire fighter on another fire was killed on that day, doing the same scouting job that I was doing. The difference was I had a lookout to warn me and he did not. Our fire burned 130,000 acres that day. I got moved to another part of the fire near the old gold-mining town. In the old cemetery there was and an interpretive sign telling how all 26 had died. Every one of them died from disease or gunshots. That's a tough way to make a living!

MISSOURI FIRES

A Labor of Love

When I was still in Blue Springs in my first year with MDC, I was asked to go to Clinton, Missouri to help on a large fire. It was an arson fire that had been intentionally set in 24 places. I hooked up in Clinton with a veteran firefighter named Arlen. We drove out to the fire and it looked to me that the whole world was on fire. We joined up with a crew and began building a containment line. The sun was going down as we completed this piece of fire line and had contained a portion of the fire. Arlen and I got in his truck and drove to a hill where we could see most of the remaining fire. Arlen lit up his pipe and gazed on the huge glow of fire. He took a big draw on his pipe and then said "Man, I love this." I looked at the fire and could not understand what he was talking about. All I could see was an endless job. Arlen went to his truck and pulled out a small brown sack called a fire ration. That was the first time I realized that I had not eaten all day. He only had one fire ration, so he started divvying up its contents.

He opened the can of beanie weenies and spread the weenies out on a piece of cardboard so he could make sure we both had the same amount of them. Next, he poured out the canned fruit contents and divided up the number of cherries. There was an odd number of cherries, and he took the extra cherry because that was his favorite. After eating the two-course meal, we climbed back into the truck and met up with the fire crew. Over the next two days of fire suppression, the words "Man I love this" kept running through my head. We finally got the fire out and the mop up completed. I again looked over the large black scar and considered the hard work and team effort required to get to this point. The fire was 2,500 acres in size. I thought to myself, what an accomplishment, what a team effort. I thought I might like this too!

Plan B

A lady walked into my office, introduced herself and sat down. She told me that she saw a man set a fire and then told me his name. We had suspected this guy concerning annual fires near his house. The fires were always set on property owned by a man living in New Mexico. This property bordered the suspected arsonist's property.

I told her about a program that the Missouri Department of Conservation had, called Operation Forest Arson. I told her that this program gives rewards for turning in arsonists. I asked her if she would be willing to testify in court what she saw. She quickly said, "No, he lives too close to me and he is not a nice man." I told her thanks for letting us know and that I would keep our conversation confidential. After she left, I got an idea. I sat down in front of my computer and began typing a letter to the arsonist. I wrote, "I saw you set a fire on property you do not own. I did not turn you in this time. If I ever see you set another fire, I will turn you in and receive a reward from the Missouri Department of Conservation."

I mailed the anonymous letter that same day. We never had a fire on that property again!

ONLY BONNY

We were dispatched to a fire on the monastery property. Stan, Burley, Avery, and I arrived at the fire which was burning very hot thanks to tall grass and red cedar. The plan was to begin plowing off O Highway and continue plowing a control line with the bulldozer around the fire in a horseshoe pattern and tie back into O Highway. We began plowing and it was slow going because the wind kept blowing fire brands over the control line. We would quickly put them out before they got big. It took us about an hour to get around this flank and continue back toward the highway. (The horseshoe pattern is how we tie into something that will not burn or as we call it, the anchor. You start at an anchor and end at an anchor. In this case our anchor was O highway.) I stopped because I thought I had heard a motor running ahead of us. Sure enough, Brother Boniface (Bonny) came walking out of the smoke. He had no eye protection, nor fire resistant clothing. He had a leaf rake in his hand and a backpack blower on his back. His hair stood on end and he was drenched with sweat. He had stuffed toilet paper in his ears because he had no ear protection from the loud blower. The paper was sticking at least three inches out of his ears and the ends of the toilet paper were burnt and still smoking! The good Brother put out the whole east flank all by himself. I asked him if he needed a drink of water and he said, "Not until the mop up is done." He turned around and walked out of sight. He is quite a guy.

ROCKET'S RED GLARE

It was 10:00 p.m. and I got a call about another fire on the monastery land. I called Stan and Burley and we drove to the abbey. We were crossing Bryant Creek and saw some teenagers shooting bottle rockets from the bottom of the bluff to the top of the bluff. We also saw a large glow on top of the bluff. We contacted the Sheriff's office and told them what was going on.

I mentioned earlier that the monastery was 3000 acres. There are few interior roads on the property. We drove up the hill to the abbey, gathered our fire tools and took off on a one-mile hike into the dark. We did have a large glow to guide us. As we were walking, we noticed the glow getting smaller. When we finally arrived at the fire, there was Brother Boniface with his leaf blower. He had nearly put out the fire by himself. I suggested to him that because he had done the hard part, let us do the mop up and for him to go back to bed. He did not argue at all, instead turned around and began walking back to the abbey with no flashlight. God's own firefighter, that Bonny!

MASON DIXON LINE

I received a call from the Sheriff's Office concerning a fire on the state line. It was after dark and no wind, so I thought I would size it up before calling for more assistance. I arrived at the fire and discovered that the Arkansas Department of Forestry had sent four firefighters to this same fire. It was not burning very hot so I suggested that they take the left flank, and I would take the right flank and I would meet them somewhere on the other side. I worked for quite a while and figured out that this was a bigger fire than I had thought. I continued to put the same flame out with my leaf rake and about an hour later I came to the point where I started from. Arkansas went home! That was the last time I almost worked with my neighbors to the south.

CANNOT MAKE THIS UP!

Stan and I were dispatched to a fire south of Ava, on a property that we had been to before. The 40 acres was owned by an old man (Rufus) and his grown son Jed. Both men were widely known to be heavy drinkers. Stan and I arrived at the farm and could see smoke rising on the east side of the property. When we knocked on the door, we found no one in the house. We grabbed our fire gear and headed toward the smoke. We sized up the fire as slow-moving with flames only about three to five inches tall. We walked up a hill along the fire's edge and at the top of the hill sound asleep against a tree, with whiskey bottle in hand, was ole Rufus. Stan yelled, "RUFUS WAKE UP!" He was so drunk and startled that he jumped up and then rolled down the hill on top of the fire's edge. He virtually snuffed out that portion of the fire without getting hurt. He proved that "Stop, Drop and Roll" really works.

AN INSENSITIVE BAT

Stan and I were called to a fire located on the property of a religious cult in northern Douglas County. When we arrived, we met up with five men and a teenage girl. They had fought fire before and were building a fire break with leaf rakes. Stan and I jumped into the line, and the eight of us were building a wide, dirt line. I was working next to the young girl when I saw her bend down and pick up a small brown bat that had been hiding in the leaves. I told her that was not a good Idea, but her motherly instinct took over. She was looking at the bat when her dad yelled at her to get to work. She immediately put the bat in her front shirt pocket and went back to raking. I told her that was a bad idea again, but she ignored me and went back to raking leaves. It only took about 30 seconds before she gave out a painful scream as the "cute little bat" bit down on a specific female body part lying behind the shirt pocket.

Her motherly instinct was no longer there, and she shifted to survival mode. She dug the bat out of the pocket and threw it as far as possible. Her dad was at the end of the line and had no idea why she was acting the way she was. I suggested that she needed first aid because bats carry diseases. Fearing I was going to administer first aid, she screamed at me, "Don't touch me!!!" I kindly told her that she needed to tell her dad what happened. She just kept right on working, saying nothing, but mad as a hornet.

THE UNDERDOG

It was Stan and I again heading to a hot fire on a bad fire weather day. As we pulled into the driveway the landowner pointed to a doghouse that was about to catch fire, with a Rottweiler chained to the house. Stan immediately started up his water unit and put out the part of the fire that was threatening the dog. It was all blackened ash around the doghouse, so he was no longer in danger from the fire.

The rest of the fire was back in the woods, so Stan and I grabbed a rake and a blower and attacked the fire. We spent several hours extinguishing the fire in the woods. We made it back to the homeowner and told him it was out but that he should keep an eye on it as it could rekindle. We got in our truck and started to leave when Stan jumped out of his truck. The poor dog that Stan had worked so diligently to save from the fire had crawled under his truck, seeking shade, and Stan ran over him. The landowner took the blame for letting the dog off the leash but that did not make him feel any better. This was the only fire fatality I had ever had, in 40 years of fighting fire.

RAILROAD FIRES

We used to have several fires that were started by the brakes of railroad cars and engines. When they hit the brakes, the metal shoes and metal rails would spark fires in the near-by grasses. We got a fire call from a landowner whose property adjoined the railroad tracks in Oregon County. Because of his narrow driveway, we had to drive the bulldozer (Macky was my bulldozer driver) across the fairways of a golf course. This was not popular with the golfers. We arrived at the fire and there were a dozen junk cars that had just enough gas to cause a small explosion. Piles of household trash were on fire near the junk cars. The house was a safe distance away. Using the dozer to circle the fire with a constructed dirt fire break, we quickly had the fire under control. I asked the landowner how the fire started. He said the train started the fire. He continued to say that they set a fire on him every year. I just needed to send them a letter with my name and the date of the fire and they would send him $1,400 for the damages. I walked to my truck shaking my head. Apparently, he did not watch the news on TV. The railroad was on strike and there had not been a train through there in two weeks. His "cash cow" may now be dead.

AERIAL DETECTION

In the 1980's we had many wildfires in the Ozarks. People started fires to kill ticks, burn trash, or because they were mad at their neighbor, or mad because they couldn't hunt on a property. Another very common reason was, "my daddy did it, my gramps did it, so I do it."

We would contract annually with a pilot to fly aerial fire detection. After a little training, the pilot could tell the difference between a wildfire and a controlled prescribed fire. Not all pilots are created equal. In the early days before radio use, pilots would put locations of fires in a canister with a note and drop the canister near a firefighter. Even after the pilots used radios for communicating messages, the radios were not always dependable. A pilot once flew so low he yelled to the firefighters that there was another fire behind them. When we had a new pilot, someone would have to ride with him until he understood how to read a map and assess a fire. We generally only had the planes fly detection when the fire danger was high due to low humidity, or high winds. Winds of 20 to 30 mph on the ground are going to be 40 to 60 mph in the air. Unfortunately for the pilot, that guarantees a rough flight. Those with military background were easy to train, others, not so easy. I flew with a pilot that gave flying lessons as his only experience. He was not used to flying in high winds and several times he screamed when the wind gusted. I was used to the high winds but not a screaming pilot.

I flew with a retired naval pilot that was enjoyable, at least for me. We were flying and it was a slow day. I was looking out the right side of the plane when the pilot said, "Take the wheel." I whipped my head around and said, "What did you say?" He repeated, "Take the wheel, I need to take a leak." He pulled out a hospital pee bottle and I grabbed the wheel. I did not realize how sensitive the wheel was. I flinched too much, and the nose jerked up. It was just enough to dump the contents of the pee bottle into the pilot's lap. After a few choice words he straightened up the plane and said very little the rest of the day.

There was a private pilot that lived north of us about 30 minutes. Whenever he heard the local fire department going to a wild-land fire, he would fill up the water tank in his plane and help out by dropping water on the fire. He did not have the needed radio frequency so often the guys on the ground got a good shower because they didn't know he was coming. This went on for two fire seasons and then we found out a critical detail that forced us to ask him to quit. He had a plane on which the water tank was filled by scooping water out of lakes and reservoirs. But this guy's water source was the city sewage lagoon.

One year we had several fires in the Federal Mark Twain National Forest. Arsonists would set fires every time the Federal Government did something unpopular. Taxes go up, set a fire. Wrong president was elected, set a fire. One guy got caught setting fire and he of course had a reason. He did not want the Forest Service to cut down trees, so he burned them down! makes perfect sense.

One fire season we had our fire detection plane flying over a US Forest Service property. The pilot radioed in to the dispatcher that he just witnessed someone setting a fire (right place at the right time). A fire crew was dispatched to the location given by the pilot. In the meantime, the pilot followed the arsonist at a high elevation so as not to be detected. The arsonist drove his pickup truck straight to a small house about 15 miles from the fire. The pilot gave the dispatcher the location of the house and said he would keep circling in case the suspect left. Both state and federal law enforcement showed up within 15 minutes. Of course, the guy initially denied any wrongdoing until the agents took him outside and showed him the circling airplane. The agents asked him why he set the fire. He was mad at the government because they had just arrested his brother for cutting walnut logs off federal land. He was convicted of arson in federal court and was reunited with his brother. Misery loves company.

I Feel Good

One fire season had been especially tough. We had several days of very low humidity which is a key factor in fire behavior. When the humidity is 25% or less, the moisture evaporates from the leaves and grasses. All it takes is an ignition source to create a big fire. In Missouri an ignition source can be any of the following: fireworks, burning trash, burning grass and leaves, hot vehicle brakes, faulty vehicle exhaust systems, trains, electric fences and all too often, arson. We had gone several weeks without a day off. The Ava work team was dragging into the office, sipping coffee, and eating donuts. Stan was the last one to arrive and he stepped through the door attempting to imitate the singer James Brown singing "I Feel Good." He was quickly silenced by flying donuts and harsh words. Before Stan could get his coffee poured, we got a fire call. The landowner on the phone said his land was on fire and the fire was heading toward the barn. When we arrived, the barn was burning and beyond saving. We were almost done putting the fire out and we got a call on the radio telling us to go to a fire on the Alford property. This 5,000-acre forest was not new to arson fire as the owner did not allow hunting and irresponsible hunters annually retaliated with arson. We left two firefighters to finish this fire and the rest of the core team drove their trucks and the bulldozer to the large forest fire. The fire was already 40 acres and moving fast up a steep hill. The plan was for Francis to drive the bulldozer around the fire with the plow down to create a five-foot wide, dirt firebreak. Stan, Billy and I followed the bulldozer to put out any fires that jumped over the plowed fire line. We were making good progress, and then trouble appeared. The bulldozer was on a side hill and began to roll over. Fortunately, a tree stopped it from rolling completely over. Francis walked away unhurt but shaken. We now had to complete the fire break using hand tools which is significantly slower. We contacted dispatch to request another bulldozer and they replied that all regional bulldozers were on other fires and they would send one when it became available. Daylight turned to dark and the bright glow from the fire guided our path. We had not eaten since the morning donuts. The sun was rising as we finally made it all around the fire. William arrived with a bulldozer in tow. He stepped out of the truck carrying a homemade cherry pie. It was an awful sight watching four hungry men consume a cherry pie with no plates or utensils. Sleep deprivation affects people in two ways. They either are mad or slap happy and the two do not get along. While we were inhaling the pie, William used his bulldozer to upright ours. He then drove his dozer around the fire to make sure the fire was safely out. We climbed into our vehicles and began the 40-minute drive to the shop. We had been working for 43 hours by the time we pulled into our parking lot. There was an unknown MDC vehicle parked there. I walked into the office and Fred from Jefferson City had come down to see how fire season was going. While Fred and I were talking, Stan was completing the fire report on top of a truck hood. Fred wanted to take me to lunch, so I was obligated to go. I turned to tell Stan where I was going and he had fallen asleep, standing up, and his head laying on the hood and his face laying in a pool of saliva. I just shook my head and walked out to Fred's vehicle. The next morning everyone in the office agreed that Stan could no longer sing James Brown again.

In 2000 I wrote an article for the Missouri Conservationist talking about one of the Western fires I had worked. With their permission I am sharing that story in this book.

FIRE FIGHTING WESTERN STYLE

Publish Date:
May 02, 2000
Revised Date:
Nov 05, 2010
Tim Stanton

*Every year, when big fires advance up the west coast
toward northern California, Idaho, Oregon and
Washington, experienced Missouri firefighters start
gearing up -- mentally and physically.*

It is not that the western fires are any threat to Missouri. We have our own fire problems here. However, most years the Conservation Department, by request of the U.S. Forest Service, sends one or two 20-person crews, including support and super- visory people, to help fight western fires.

Firefighting can get into your blood, and that's part of the reason why people volunteer to leave home for three weeks. There is an adrenaline rush from watching a fire race from treetop to treetop and even more of a thrill from being able to stop the fire's advance. In a way, it's a test of self confidence in the face of Mother Nature's worst behavior.

Western fire duty allows Conservation Department personnel to learn and refine their wildfire suppression skills. These skills pay obvious dividends during Missouri's spring and fall fire seasons.

I was on standby for being called to fight western fires one summer a few years ago. I wasn't sure whether I would be going or when, but knowing the call could come at any time, I kept my bags packed and stayed in fire-fighting shape by running every day at the local high school track.

Finally, the call came. Tom Ronk, the Conservation Department's fire program supervisor asked me if I could be at the Forest 44 Conservation Area near St. Louis at 5:00 a.m. the next morning. From there our group would travel to Oregon to fight fires.

After several phone calls, some last-minute packing, and a ceremonial haircut, I was in route to St. Louis.

Many of the crew members were already at Forest 44 when I arrived.

Some were organizing their equipment; others were trading stories from their last trip. All were anxious, but the veterans knew how not to look too excited, as the rookies nervously checked and rechecked their gear.

Crew supervisors, squad bosses and crew members held frequent meetings to make sure everyone was mentally and physically prepared to fight fire for 21 days. We held a fire shelter practice session to ensure that every one of us knew how to use this life saving equipment. Supervisors also weighed our gear. No one could board the plane with over 55 pounds of clothing and protective equipment. After we received the final briefing on our roles and assignments, the group loaded on buses headed to Lambert-St. Louis International Airport.

Fire camps often have unusual names taken from people, topographic features or someone's wild imagination. The Forest Service sent us to a group of three fires near Granite, Oregon called the Bull Complex. They included the Bull, Summit and Tower fires. The three fires combined were relatively small by western standards, totaling less than 4,000 acres.

Support personnel were setting up the base camp when we arrived. We were among the first five crews there. A meal caterer and shower unit had been set up, and a communication unit, supply depot, finance and time section, security unit and the all-important commissary arrived later. This had the potential to become a big fire, and in one week the camp grew to over 2,000 firefighters and support personnel.

My crew's first assignment was to go to the Bull Fire with two other crews. Our leaders told us to mop up a burned area that had jumped a road the day before. A bulldozer made a line around this "slop-over," but there were still logs burning near the control line.

Mopping up is to firefighting what playing offensive guard is to football. There is little excitement or glory. It is essential, hard work. We were to snuff out any remains of the fire using hand tools and water from a fire truck.

After several days of similar assignments, the commander of the camp assigned us to climb seven miles and 1,000 vertical feet to another site. The rocky ascent took us over half a day, before we finally linked up with another firefighting crew.

We spent the rest of the day holding a control line, trying to keep the fire from jumping over it. This was done with a watchful eye, several helicopter drops and quick reflexes. Near sunset we hiked another two miles (mostly uphill) to a spike camp. A helicopter lowered a cargo net full of supplies, such as bottled water, sleeping bags, granola bars and toilet paper.

In the base camp we slept under a piece of plastic on the ground, which is good living compared to spike camp, where you are clinging to the edge of a steep mountain. Helicopters and trucks delivered meals in plastic foam coolers. One evening we ran out of paper plates and used cut-up pieces of cardboard to eat taco salad on. There were no privies, only our shovels.

When we ate dinner that night an enormous orange and red glow to the north lit the moonless night. More spectacular than the Fourth of July, the fiery cloud devoured acres of timber. The center of the cloud pulsated like a beating heart. Radio traffic said the humidity was 19 percent at 10:00 p.m.

The Tower Fire was making a run toward the Bull Complex Base Camp. It had grown 20,000 acres in one day and had moved six miles in 2 hours. The top of the cloud was over 30,000 feet and was creating its own weather, with lightning and 20 mph winds out of the east. Everywhere else had 5 mph winds out of the south.

The order came over the radio to evacuate the base camp because the Tower Fire was only two miles away. In all the chaos, they had forgotten about our spike camp.

Our division leader called the supervisors in the spike camp together. We made the decision to hang tough where we were. Spike camp was near an old gold mine within an open rocky ridge. Because there was little fuel for the fire, we felt safe. We posted lookouts throughout the night with radio linkage back to the camp. It was a restless night, and everyone slept with one eye open and their radio on.

I was one of the first to awake in the morning and found the cloud had died down somewhat and was in about the same location. I heard a Missouri crew member wake up and say, "I'm still alive," which drew a chuckle of relief from the rest of the crew. The breakfast menu included boxed cereal and granola bars that came in with the taco salad.

The operations section was extremely surprised, embarrassed, and apologetic when we finally reached them by radio. They told us to work our way back to the drop unit, where buses would take us to the new base camp at Meadowbrook. It took us all day to reach the new camp. We were amazed that an entire camp of 2,000, along with all support facilities, had moved 25 miles overnight and was functioning as if nothing had happened.

After two and a half weeks of digging in the dirt, washing down ash, sleeping on the ground and waiting in line for food and toilets, we couldn't help thinking about home. When a bus took us to the Pendleton airport for a chartered plane to St. Louis, the Bull and Summit fires were almost out, but the Tower Fire was still going.

Mixed emotions ran through every crew member. It was good to be going home again, but the strong bond that had been formed with my crew members would soon be broken. We had done what we were expected to do and helped fight the fire, but until next summer we would have to tell the story of the "big one" that got away.

FIERY FOE

Oh, wildfire my worthy adversary, we cross paths again this year. Despite years of confrontation, I still honor you with respect and fear.

You never will be eliminated, and time after time you return. Leaving me to wonder, how much this time will you burn?

We have some things in common, as we both hunger, breathe and live. We both require victory, and will our all to give.

You are born through energy above or born through ignorance below. You may begin as a simple spark, but oh how quickly you grow.

Your spirit rises high, as you boast among the cloud. This is how I find you, standing arrogantly so proud.

Your omnivorous appetite will consume all things that stand in your way. I must deny you nourishment, to be victorious by end of day.

For now, I have won the battle, but there is no end to the war. We both will return for the challenge, and the uncertainties in store.

Tim Stanton

YOU MIGHT BE A FORESTER IF...

You use a prescribed burn on your lawn rather than a mower.
You think a chainsaw is a musical instrument.

Your neighbor keeps losing trees, while you always have plenty of firewood.

You say soil and insects instead of dirt and bugs.

Latin is a part of your everyday language.

You can spell the sound a chainsaw makes.

After taking Philosophy, you still don't know the answer to the question: "If a tree falls in the woods and no one is around to hear it, does it make a sound?"

You still cannot understand why there are no tuxedos made of plaid flannel.

You brush three times a day and still cannot get the green off your teeth.

(Credit for the above goes to University of Missouri Forestry Club.)

It has been a crazy ride!

I must thank Missouri Department of Conservation for having faith in me to do the job requested and giving me the opportunity to see the environmental wonders of Missouri and every state west of Missouri.

Thank you, Chloeta, for the opportunity to work Natural Resource Management with you and for taking the chance on this book.

I have sincerest gratitude to Diana, Nichole, Valerie, and Gwen for the assistance with writing, editing, writing some more, and editing again. I know I was a challenge, and you were the best.

Thanks too, Ric Buchanan for pictures and unwavering friendship.

Location: John Day, Oregon
Photo Credit: Unknown

Mark Masters of Chloeta, unknown firefighter,
and me working fire in Nebraska.
Photo Credit: Chloeta

Prescribed fire in Minnesota
Photo Credit: Unknown

Back where it all started. Burr Oak, Blue Springs, MO
Photo Credit: Gwen Stanton

SOME INTERESTING STUFF I FOUND WALKING DOWN MEMORY LANE!

My offer letter from MDC.
January 4, 1980
Supervision
Missouri Department of Conservation
PO Box 180
Jefferson City, MO 65102
Larry R. Gale, Director
Jerry J. Presley, State Forester
Lawrence L. Lackamp, District Forester

We are going to employ Tim Stanton, a graduate of the University of Missouri School of Forestry, Fisheries & Wildlife, as a temporary employee at the beginning salary for a PM 1 level. Stanton will be assigned to the Kansas City Forest District and will be under your immediate supervision. You should plan on working him on a full time basis (similar to Rhoades) and we will pay Stanton's salary out of our Central Office administrative account. It will be necessary for to process the necessary monthly payroll information on Stanton.

By copy of this memorandum I am asking Stanton to contact you by telephone (816/228-3766) to arrange a suitable starting date. You should prorate Stanton's monthly salary over the total days he works during January. He will probably be available to begin work immediately.

JJP/ms
Cc: Osal B. Capps
    Kerwin Hafner
    Bob Massengale
    Clell Solomon
    Tim Stanton

INTERESTING FIND FOR THE FEDERAL DEPARTMENT OF AGRICULTURE (COWBOY DAYS) BEFORE MDC EXISTED.

Series No 4
Apr., 1908
Sheet 1
UNITED STATES CIVIL SERVICE COMMISSION

———————————————

DEPARTMENTAL SERVICE – FOREST RANGER
EXAMINATION
     DEPARTMENT OF AGRICULTURE.
     Competitor must fill these blanks.

Time commenced_____. Date_____.
Examination No._____. Time finished_____. Place
of Examination_____.

N.B. – Do not write on this sheet. Blank sheets will be furnished
for the answers to the questions hereon. Number answers to cor-
respond with numbers of questions. Number consecutively the
sheets of answers to questions hereon, and write in the follow-

ing spaces the total number of such attached sheets. Number of sheets_____ Rating_____

FIRST SUBJECT – PRACTICAL QUESTIONS
Question 1.

On what Forest, or Forests do you have desire appointment as a Forest Ranger? Give general description of these Forests describing

- a. Topography, or lay of the country;
- b. The kind of Forest, giving the common names of principal merchantable trees;
- c. The logging operations, their extent and importance;
- d. The stock industry, showing the extent and nature of the range;
- e. The principal settlements in or near the Forest.
- f. In your opinion what was the main reason for creating this Forest?

Question 2.

- a. Describe in detail logging in a locality with which you are familiar, covering all operation, from felling the tree to delivery of logs at the sawmill, using all ordinary names applied to the men, operations and implements.
- b. Describe a sawmill with which you are familiar and describe how the logs are made into lumber.

Question 3.

What are the ordinary specifications of railroad ties, mining stull, lagging, fence posts? What is a cord of wood? A board foot? How are telephone poles generally measured? How are logs scaled?

Name a log scale in common use in your locality and give the contents of logs of the following sizes by this scale:

- 16 feet long and 26 inches in a diameter small end
- 18 feet long and 30 inches in diameter small end
- 24 feet long and 18 inches in diameter small end
- 12 feet long and 15 inches in diameter small end

Question 4.

What are the dimensions of a township?
Section?
Quarter section?
A forty?
A square acre?
How many links in a surveyor's chain?
How many feet?
How many chains in a mile?
How many acres in a tract of land 600 feet wide by 3960 feet long?

Question 5.

State how you would construct a 14 by 18-foot log cabin?

Question 6.

a. Enumerate the articles of food and give the amount of each which you would take with you on a two-weeks' trip in August, considering that you were entirely dependent on the supplies you took with you.

b. How many pounds can the average horse pack for six consecutive days, making 15 miles per day? How many pounds can the average man pack under the same conditions?

Question 7.

    a. Describe a method of handling range cattle in a district with which you are familiar. Range sheep.

    b. Describe by diagram four brands and four earmarks and give the name by which each is known.

Question 8.

What constitutes valid residence on homestead claim?

What are the improvement and cultivation requirements and under what conditions can patent be obtained under the Timber and Stone Act, the Desert Land Act, and the Placer Mining Laws.

Question 9.

How and for what purposes are National Forests created?

How do they affect the water flow, agriculture, lumbering, grazing, and mining?

Question 10.

What are the chief duties of a Forest Ranger?

Give a plan for protecting a specified tract of land against fire.

How would you fight a fire on this tract if it had a good start?

SECOND SUBJECT – FIELD TEST

INSTRUCTIONS TO THE EXAMINER – Under "Ratings" the examiner will give the rating which, in his opinion, the competitor is entitled in each test, considering the fitness of the competitor, skill and ability shown, on the following basis: Very poor, 40 per cent or less; poor, 50 per cent; tolerable, 60 per cent; fair,

70 per cent; good, 80 per cent; excellent, 90 per cent; perfect, 100 percent. Under "Remarks" the reasons for very high or very low ratings should be given, and any facts noted which may bear upon the rating given or affect the value of the competitor's service to the Government.

Question 1.

Saddle and bridle a horse.

Ride a quarter of a mile and return (*a*) at a trot, (*b*) at a gallop.

Time and manner of saddling and unsaddling to be taken into consideration by the examiner.

Question 2.

Pack a horse with a tent, two blankets, one-man cook outfit, axe, and shovel, and sufficient grain or provisions to make an entire pack weigh 150 pounds. No panniers to be used. Any satisfactory hitch to be accepted. (Rate on familiarity, neatness, and dispatch and also experience as determined by oral questions. Competitors should not be allowed to watch examination of other competitors.)

Question 3.

Estimate by pacing the distance around a triangular tract of not less than one-half mile, giving distance in rods, yards, and feet. (After all estimates have been submitted examiner will measure exact distance with tape or chain. The route should not be less than one-half mile in length.)

Question 4.

Set up a compass and allowing for the variation given by the examining officer, indicate east, north 25 degrees west, south 50 degrees east. Take the bearing of a designated object and give the compass reading. (Allow only a reasonable length of time for the applicant to complete this test. Rate on quickness, accuracy, familiarity, and experience as determined by oral questions. No competitor should be allowed to watch the examination of other competitors.)

Question 5.

Run a compass line around a designated area and read and record the courses, allowing for the variation as given by the examining officer. (Lay out a five-sided irregular figure, with sides between 100 and 200 feet in length, setting proper poles or stakes at each angle. Allow only a reasonable length of time for the applicant to complete this test. Rate on quickness, accuracy, familiarity, and experience as determined by oral questions. No competitor should be allowed to watch the examination of other competitors.)

I hereby certify that the above-named competitor neither gave nor received assistance during his examination, and that ratings given by me are equitable and just, to the best of my knowledge and belief.

(Signature of examiner)_____Date_____,190___

(Title) _____

_____

_____

So You Want to be a
Wild Land Fire Fighter?
(Go West Young Man or Woman)

Being a wild land fire fighter encompasses a crew, twenty unique skilled individuals, each with duties and tasks all chosen by the Missouri Department of Conservation (MDC), utilizing national guidelines. Notifying MDC of your interest in fighting wild land fires will at least result in your name on a contact list. That contact will not come until some standard training takes place.

A physical fitness test, known as the pack test, occurs annually. This test consists of walking 3 miles with forty-five pounds on your back in less than forty-five minutes. This test is a good replication of the caloric output as building a control-fire-line in forty-five minutes. An annual refresher is also required that describes with video and discussion groups the successes and failures of the previous fire season.

Now your name is on the list for upcoming fire season and you now have to acquire the standard personal equipment. This includes, hard hat, leather gloves, Nomex pants and shirt (fire resistant), leather boots with 12" top, eye protection, fire shelter, good socks, canteen or plastic water bottle, tent (in the early years this was just plastic thrown over limbs or rope), ground pad, flashlight, sleeping bag (protection from the cold), camping pillow, all contained in one gear bag that weighs less than 50 lbs. If you're lucky enough to travel with an agency they usually supply some or all the equipment. However, if there isn't a sponsor agency you are purchasing this gear by yourself. It will take you 2 to 3 trips to pay for the gear.

In the earlier days we always flew out to a fire. There were twenty person crews from three states in a federal government plane. We would fly to Boise Idaho where school buses would then transport us to the fire. Each twenty-person crew was comprised of a crew boss, assistant crew boss, three squad bosses and fifteen fire fighters. The excitement level on the bus is palpable. The new fire fighters are extremely nervous, quiet, watching the experienced fire fighters as they are making jokes and relaxed enough to start a card game. The excitement of the unknown hangs in the air, not fear, per se, but an unexplained trepidation of what lies ahead.

Fire Camp can consist of two hundred plus individuals making up one large tent city. The bigger the fire, the bigger the camp. The National Incident Management Team (NIMT) which makes all the strategic decisions are housed in several huge military tents marked with their designated role such as check-in and demobilization in one tent, operations, Geographical Information Systems (GIS), security, ground support, finance, medical, food or mess tent, shower tent, mobile laundromat, aviation with their own small airport, logistics and planning, and of course a human resource tent. There are designated crew sleeping areas safely tucked away from the busy temporary roads. These tent cities are extremely organized, well thought out, temporary cities that practice, work and travel together and are patterned after military operations. This is an impressive sight every time, even for the experienced fire fighter.

Typically, you set up your new home surrounded by your crew, a true camaraderie of a team working together to meet a common objective. It is early to bed for all, since wake up is oh-five hundred, and then off to the mess hall. The gear is prepared (sharpening of tools), sack lunches and water are packed while the crew bosses head off to get their briefing and assignment. We head off to the fire line as early as oh-six-thirty. The assignment from our crew bosses is one of the following three duties: constructing a fire break, holding a fire break or mop up.

When constructing a fire break a crew or multiple crews remove flammable fuels (such as trees, leaves, grass, etc...) to a safe distance from the fire. This construction is completed with hand tools, bull dozers, chain saws and fire retardant or a combination of all tactics. Surprisingly, dynamite is also used to clear trees and debris ahead of an oncoming fire. The objective is to remove a swath free of combustible fuel before the fire arrives. The width of the fire line is determined by the height of the flames. The higher the flames the wider the fire break. The break can be as small as three feet wide and as large as thirty feet wide! If these tactics don't work the crew falls back and tries it again.

Holding a fire break is actually fighting fire with fire. At a safe distance from the oncoming larger fire, a control line is established. After building a fire break, a small fire is set on the same side of the line as the larger fire. The desired effect is to burn out all the flammable fuels from the break to the larger fire. When the two fires come together it burns out because there is no more ground debris to fuel the fire. The crew mans the line to make sure the hold lasts and no sparks ignite the surface on the other side of the break. The holding of the break can last hours or even days.

And then there is mop-up. It is exactly as it sounds. It is dirty, smoky, monotonous, but necessary to keep the fire from reigniting and jumping over the control line. The fire can actually burn in the root system of a tree and come back up on the other side of the break. The trees can reignite and blow sparks over the break as well. Mop-up can take several days of dirty work in ash to keep the fire at bay.

The day crews, due to safety hazards of working in the dark, typically work sixteen-hour shifts, seven days a week. Upon return to camp, there comes a decision based on individual preference: food, shower, or sleep. If sleep is your priority, you go straight to bed in order to get the much desired eight hours of sleep. The other two options require a waiting period of probably an hour. Waiting in line to shower is the worst. It is another hour of standing, waiting, just to stand in a shower. (The degree of dirt build-up became a red badge of courage.) For me, with exhaustion beating me down, the shower didn't seem so important. Waiting for food made more sense if I was going to wait for something. A final choice may be standing in line in order to use one of the phones to call home. That choice came up usually once a week rather than daily. No matter the decision, it all came down to how much sleep you required to get the job done.

For a crew this goes on for 14 days and then they either go home or have two days off. An interesting factor, when a crew loses two members from injury, quitting, or have family issues back home, the entire crew has to go home if the members aren't replaced.

I did enjoy the challenge of fighting these wild land fires. I was able to work my way up to crew boss, and then safety officer came later as I acquired more skills over the years. The work either gets in your blood or not. It requires a work ethic beyond description, a determination and desire that I carried for thirty years.

Camp Day 1
Photo Credit: Greg Hoss

Photo Credit: Greg Hoss

Fire Crew
Photo Credit: Greg Hoss

Waiting for Orders
Photo Credit: Greg Hoss

Line Crew
Photo Credit: Greg Hoss

Established Fire Lines
Photo Credit: Greg Hoss

Photo Credit: Greg Hoss

Quick Lunch Break with a view.
Photo Credit: Greg Hoss

Working the hand tools.
Photo Credit: Greg Hoss

Fires can get out of control quickly.
Photo Credit: Chloeta

Fighting fire with fire.
Photo Credit: Rick Buchanon

Credit: Rick Buchanon

Establishing a fire break.
Photo Credit: Greg Hoss

Safety Officer in my later years.
Photo Credit: Rick Buchanon

CPSIA information can be obtained
at www.ICGtesting.com
Printed in the USA
BVHW020748301221
625045BV00024B/4

9 7 8 1 9 5 3 9 1 2 2 9 9